A Guide to
Hopi
Katsina
Dolls

Kent McManis

*Photographs
by Robin Stancliff*

Rio Nuevo Publishers
Tucson, Arizona

FRONTISPIECE:

*Yotsi´katsina
(Apache katsina) by
Cecil Calnimptewa.
This katsina appears
in nightdances and
represents the spirit
of the Apache people
(courtesy private
collection).*

Rio Nuevo Publishers
An imprint of Treasure Chest Books
P.O. Box 5250
Tucson, AZ 85703-0250
(520) 623-9558

ISBN 1-887896-17-1
Editor: Ronald J. Foreman
Designer: William Benoit,
          Simpson & Convent
Printed in Korea
10 9 8 7 6 5 4 3 2 1

Contents

Acknowledgments

As always, I accomplished this book with the help of many individuals. Most importantly, I want to express my love and admiration to my wife Laurie for all her patience and hard work on this project and for putting up with me all these years. Thanks to my father, Larry, for giving me my first katsina doll at age three. (Yes, I still have it, although its nose and most of its paint are long gone.) Bruce McGee, a true gentleman and one of the nicest people in the Native American arts business, has been extraordinarily helpful. Always amazing Robin Stancliff deserves special recognition for her beautiful images of the dolls. I especially want to acknowledge the artists whose creations are featured here: They are among the finest katsina carvers working today, and I only wish time and space permitted me to include examples from all the other Hopi artists whose work I admire. To them and the many other Hopi people who have graciously shared their knowledge, vision, and art with me over the years, I say "Kwakwháy."

Katsina vs. Kachina:
A note about spelling, pronunciation, and plural forms

The term kachina (kah-chee-nah) has long been used by outsiders to refer to any of the hundreds of spiritual beings central to Hopi religious life as well as to the dolls that depict them. However, according to the Hopi, katsina (kahts-ee-nah) is more correct and preferred. Also, whereas in English the plural of kachina would be kachinas, in the Hopi language the plural of katsina is formed by adding "m": katsinam.

Introduction

The Cloud People

On a warm July morning many years ago, several friends and I stood atop one of the Hopi mesas in northeastern Arizona. We were privileged to witness the stately and sacred "Home Dance," which the Hopi call Niman or Nimaniwu. Before us, a line of resplendent Hemiskatsinam formed. These spirit beings moved to the thundering rhythm that three different kneeling katsinmamant, or katsina maidens, rasped out on huge gourds. As the katsinam danced and sang their throaty song, the clattering tortoise shell rattles tied to their legs and crisp-sounding gourd hand rattles combined to create a din like driving hail or rain. Colorful, terraced tablita head-dresses—showing plants, fertility, and rain symbols—swayed gently above the Hemiskatsinam, evoking a line of cumulus clouds.

At that moment, my attention was drawn away from this remarkable scene to the still-snowcapped San Francisco Peaks, a katsinam home sixty miles to the southwest. Billowing clouds were beginning to form a straight line between the distant mountains and the Hopi mesa where the "Cloud People" were performing this ancient ritual. Prophetically, the thunderheads were coming to retrieve the katsinam after their half-year stay at Hopi, where everything in life is imbued with the spiritual and sacred.

Chapter 1

The Hopi and the Katsinam

The Hopi (literally translated as a person who behaves in a polite and peaceful way) are a communal farming people who reside in stone and adobe villages on and near three mesas in northeastern Arizona. Sixteenth century Spanish explorers, who were the first Europeans to encounter the Hopi and other sedentary Indians of the Southwest, referred to these inhabitants as Pueblo, or town, dwellers. The katsinam are integral to the religious life of most Pueblo peoples of the Southwest, but the Hopi pantheon is by far the largest. The Hopi also are one of the very few Pueblo nations whose artisans carve katsina dolls for sale. In addition, they produce beautiful hand-coiled pottery, coiled and wicker baskets, complex overlay jewelry, and weavings.

More than nine thousand Hopi live on a 1.5 million-acre reservation that encompasses a dozen villages. Waalpi, Hanoki (also known as Tewa Village), Sitsomovi, and Polacca are located on or near easternmost First Mesa. Songoopavi, Musangnuvi, and Supawlavi are situated on Second Mesa. Hotvela, Paaqavi, Kiqötsmovi, and Orayvi are on or near Third Mesa, while Mùnqapi is located further west, near the Navajo community of Tuba City. The glossary and pronunciation guides included in this book reflect the fact that the sound of certain Hopi words will vary according to which mesa a Hopi speaker calls home.

Hopiland is an arid, sandy, high desert. Rainfall is scanty and the growing season is relatively short. It takes concerted effort, great skill, a lot of faith, and more than a little luck for people to survive in this relatively harsh environment. The ingenious Hopi have prospered by developing hardy strains of corn, beans, and squash, which they cultivate in sand dunes that capture and retain runoff from the mesas above. But they also believe that, their best efforts notwithstanding, their survival as a people depends upon maintaining proper relationships with inhabitants of the spiritual realm, for only the katsinam have the power to bring rain and bestow blessings.

We can't be sure exactly when the people we now know as the Hopi first arrived in the American Southwest. There are deserted, prehistoric pueblo ruins scattered throughout the Four Corners region that date back at least fifteen centuries, and the people who built these impressive structures clearly have cultural links to the Hopi and other Pueblo peoples. Hopi oral tradition maintains that their ancestors passed through three previous worlds, all of which were destroyed by one natural disaster or another. The ancestral Hopi ultimately came up into this Fourth World through the Sípàapuni, the place of emergence that tradition says is located in the Grand Canyon. Only after a series of great migrations did the Hopi people finally arrive at their current homeland. The Hopi villages of Awat´ovi and Orayvi were occupied as early as the twelfth century, and Orayvi has the distinction of being one of the oldest continually inhabited communities in the United States.

Early representations of the katsinam are quite extensive. Examples of katsina imagery in rock art date back to the eleventh or twelfth centuries. Stone katsina-like figures appeared as early as the 1100s, while similar, carved wooden figures have been found dating to about 1300. Hopi pottery exhibits katsina designs from around 1300 on.

In the summer of 1540, the residents of Awat´ovi at the base of First Mesa were surprised to see a contingent of heavily armored men approaching from the southeast. These Spanish explorers, led by Pedro de Tovar, were mounted on horses, which the Hopi had never seen before. Tovar was an adjutant to Francisco Vásquez de Coronado, who was leading what would prove to be a fruitless expedition to find the fabled Seven Cities of Gold. Vásquez de Coronado had dispatched Tovar and his men to find the Hopi villages, which the people of the Zuni pueblo had said lay to the northwest, in hopes of discovering the riches his expedition had failed to find at Zuni.

The Spanish did not attempt to establish a permanent presence among the Hopi until 1629, when Franciscan friars began building a mission at Awat´ovi. The missionaries were determined to Christianize all the Pueblo peoples and force them to abandon their own, "pagan" religions. In their zeal, the priests destroyed many Pueblo religious artifacts and shrines and suppressed the katsina ceremonies. In 1680, the people of the various Pueblos united to drive the Spanish colonists and missionaries from their midst. The Hopi murdered the Franciscans and destroyed their missions.

The Pueblo Revolt was overwhelmingly successful but short-lived: In 1692, forces led by Governor Diego de Vargas reasserted control over "Nuevo México." Fearing reprisals from the Spanish, many Tewa-speaking Indians from the Rio Grande pueblos fled to Hopi. There they established their own villages, including Hanoki, which also is known as Tewa Village. Many of these refugees later chose to return to their own pueblos.

In 1700, the residents of Awat´ovi broke with the rest of Hopi and welcomed the Franciscan missionaries back.

This decision enraged their neighbors, who rose up and leveled the entire town, killing both Spanish and Hopi alike. Awat´ovi would forever lie in ruins, and the Spanish would never regain a foothold among the Hopi. Indeed, civil Spanish authorities basically gave up on Hopi, determining it to be too far away to be dominated from the Palace of the Governors in Santa Fe.

Americans first appeared in Hopi territory in the 1830s and began arriving in larger numbers after the United States took control of New Mexico territory in 1846. Smallpox followed in their wake, and around mid-century an epidemic decimated the Hopi people. Many were forced to flee to Zuni, where each culture inevitably influenced the other. When the Hopi refugees returned, they incorporated several Zuni katsinam, including Sipiknitaqa (FIG. 1), into the Hopi pantheon.

The American newcomers were more inclined to appreciate the art and artifacts of Hopi culture, in general, and the manifestations of the katsina religion, in particular. Even so, Hopi elders initially took a dim view of selling ceremonial tithu, or katsina dolls, to outsiders. One religious leader, Tawaquoptewa of Orayvi, overcame such objections by selling dolls that combined the symbols, costumes, and features of several katsinam, as well as his own ideas. Eventually, proscriptions against the sale of authentic katsina dolls yielded to overwhelming demand, and carving katsina dolls became an acceptable and popular way for Hopi men to earn cash and trade credit.

In 1875, Thomas Keams established a trading post at Keams Canyon, east of the Hopi mesas, and began purchasing scores of katsina dolls for resale to museums as well as private collectors. Other Anglos, most notably Mennonite missionary H. R. Voth and Indian trader Frederick Volz, collected and sold dolls as well. By the time the Atchison, Topeka & Santa Fe Railway reached

FIG. 1:

Sipiknitaqa or Talmopiyàakya (Zuni Warrior katsina), artist unknown, circa 1890. This katsina is a guard who protects the other katsinam at different dances and is derived from Zuni (courtesy private collection).

northern Arizona in 1881, the practice of selling katsina dolls for the tourist trade had become commonplace. The Fred Harvey Company became a major marketer of katsina dolls, selling them to tourists through its retail outlets along the Santa Fe Railway as well as to several prestigious museums.

The federal government established a Hopi reservation in 1882 and subsequently attempted to allot to individuals lands that traditionally had been held and cultivated in common. The government also required Hopi children to attend white-run schools. These and other outside pressures created schisms among the Hopi people.

In 1906, the people of Orayvi village split when the "progressives" literally pushed the "conservatives" over a symbolic line in the sand. The "conservatives" consequently moved up to the top of Third Mesa, where they established Hotvela. When a few of these traditionalists sought to return to Orayvi, they were not welcomed back and were obliged to resettle at Paaqavi, near Hotvela. Later, the Christian Hopi living in Orayvi were banished and forced to move below Third Mesa, where they established Kiqötsmovi, which is often called "New Oraibi." An even more progressive group from Orayvi ultimately joined these outcasts.

Throughout the socially tumultuous twentieth century, and into the new millennium, the various Hopi factions have remained united by the common bonds of language, world view, and the katsinam ceremonial tradition. Even among many Christian Hopi, cultural identification with their ancestral faith remains strong.

The katsinam may be thought of as "Cloud People" because they can take on cloud form. They also are the spiritual embodiment of Hopi ancestors who now reside in the realm of the afterworld, called Maski, and serve as intermediaries between the Hopi people and their deities. Katsinam hear the prayers of the faithful and convey those supplications to the gods, who respond with blessings in the form of rain, bountiful harvests, and plentiful game animals.

The katsina ceremonial cycle begins in December and ends in July, although katsinam may appear on rare occasions during the intervening months. Each ceremony involves different and often overlapping groups of katsinam. The attire of each katsina is elaborate and highly symbolic, incorporating elements that vividly suggest the forces of nature, fertility, plants, and animals. Colors are directionally associated. Yellow represents north or northeast; blue/green points to the west or southwest; red connotes south or southeast; and white bespeaks east or northeast. Black signifies above, while grey—all colors combined—indicates below.

Hopi society is matriarchal and clan association is matrilineal, but by tradition the men are responsible for conducting religious observances. The women of the village almost never become directly involved in katsinam ceremonies, but they are responsible for preparing food for the festivities. The katsinam traditionally give katsina dolls to young Hopi girls, while boys generally receive rattles, moccasins, and miniature bows and arrows. Infant girls and boys are given putstithu or putsqatithu, which are flat dolls or cradle dolls. (FIG. 2) These dolls usually represent Hahay'i, also called Hahay'iwuuti or Hahay'imana, who embodies the Hopi ideal of motherhood. Dolls also are given to brides to denote their new, special status. Ceremonial tithu occupy places of honor in every Hopi home. To the Hopi, these family katsina dolls are neither playthings nor home decorations.

FIG. 2: *Hahay'i, Hahay'iwuuti, or Hahay'imana (a katsina mother) putstihu or putsqatihu (flat or cradle doll) by Lawrence Acadiz (courtesy Grey Dog Trading Co.).*

Hopi tithu have undergone a tremendous amount of styl-
istic change over time. Many of the first dolls purchased
by outsiders in the mid-nineteenth century were of the
flat or cradle doll (putstihu or putsqatihu) style, where
only the face shows the markings of the katsina. Arms
were only painted, and legs were rarely shown in any way.

Toward the end of the nineteenth century, Hopi carvers
began making more rounded tithu with carved legs and
arms either away from or attached to the torso. (FIG. 3)
The earliest examples of these dolls were not clothed,
but over time more began to appear with painted kilts.
(FIG. 1) Most were made entirely of carved wood, exclud-
ing the feathers, but a few were dressed with cloth in
the Zuni manner. Some artists began to experiment with
ways to suggest life and motion, if only very minimally, by
carving legs slightly bent at the knees, and by positioning
arms and legs at somewhat different angles. (FIG. 4)

After 1900, katsina dolls became increasingly popular as
items for sale to the tourist trade. Extended arms became
more common. As tourists increasingly demonstrated a
preference for dolls that could be displayed free standing
rather than as a wall hanging, carvers began to give their
dolls disproportionately large feet. They also began to use
commercial paints instead of, or in addition to, traditional

FIG. 3 (top): *Muuyawkatsina (Moon katsina), artist unknown, circa
1900. The Moon katsina helps the Hopi at night and in setting the
time for ceremonies to take place. (courtesy private collection).*

FIG. 4 (middle): *Tasapkatsina or Tasavkatsina (Navajo katsina), artist
unknown, circa 1900 (courtesy private collection).*

FIG. 5 (bottom): *Paalölöqangkatsina (Water Serpent Katsina), artist
unknown, circa 1910–20. A katsina that may come on very rare
occasions in the plaza dances. (It is not uncommon for certain katsinam to disappear or others to begin appearing.) He is considered a
powerful rain-bringer, but his katsina doll is almost never carved.
It is said he can bring too much water as well as dangerously swell
the carver's stomach. An artist was said to have died after carving
a version of this doll (courtesy private collection).*

mineral and vegetal pigments. Artists experimented with watercolors, laundry bluing, and ultimately tempera paint. (FIG. 5) Many older dolls from this period appear to have been painted in muted tones, but this effect primarily is the result of fading and handling. Tithu that have been exhibited away from direct sunlight and handled infrequently and with great care have lost little of their original vibrancy.

Except for some refinement in painting schemes and body shapes, the style of most tithu remained basically the same (FIGS. 6 and 7) until after World War II. Then, encouraged by traders and collectors, carvers began to make their tithu even less rigid and more active and lifelike. "Dressed dolls" became the norm. Makers began to adorn their

FIG. 6: *Lenangkatsina or Leenangwkatsina (Flute katsina), artist unknown, circa 1930. This katsina appears at Powamuya and with the Palhikwmana at night dances (courtesy private collection).*

FIG. 7: *Naavuktsina (Prickly Pear katsina), artist unknown, circa 1940. An old katsina who is seen in plaza dances. He was originally prayed to for an increase in the number of nopal prickly pear cacti as the Hopi at one time used the pads for food (courtesy private collection).*

FIG. 8: *Kyaro or Kyarkatsina (Parrot katsina), artist unknown, circa 1965. This katsina appears in the plaza dances and represents a prayer for more parrots and their highly prized feathers. This tihu was purchased in 1965, the first year Kyaro had appeared after a long absence from Hopi during which its doll was rarely carved (courtesy private collection).*

dolls with yarn, felt, cloth, fur, shells, plastic plants, small metal bells, and the feathers of eagles and other wild birds. The1960s Kyaro or Kyaarokatsina, or Parrot katsina, is a good example of a dressed doll from this period. (FIG. 8) Note the use of yarn, felt, and actual cornhusks.

One of the greatest challenges that confronted post-war carvers was how to create dolls that would appear to be in motion and yet be able to stand on their own. Beginning in the 1960s, it became commonplace to attach tithu, by means of nails or wooden pegs, to wooden bases to keep the dolls from toppling over.

Inexpensive "Route 66" dolls, so named because they were sold primarily through curio shops up and down that legendary highway, were a throwback to an earlier style of doll. (FIG. 9) Some of these were hand carved, but most were lathe-turned and mass-produced. As a kid in the 1950s to early 1960s, I remember buy-ing several of these dolls for 50 cents to $1.50 apiece. They also were referred to as "bellyache kachinas" because their arms were folded over the lower torsos. The other major change that gradually developed after World War II was the abandon-ment of tempera paints in favor of acrylics, and eventually oils, as well.

FIG. 9: *Sösöpa or Sösööpa (Cricket katsina), Kwewu or Kwèwkatsina (Wolf katsina), and Honànkatsina (Badger katsina), artists unknown, circa 1955–65. The Honànkatsina is associated with medicinal roots and herbs and may be seen at Angk'wa or the plaza dances (courtesy private collection).*

With the passage of federal legislation in the early 1970s, it became illegal for the Hopi to produce for commercial sale tithu that included feathers from certain migratory, threat-ened, or endangered species. This prohibition, more than any other single factor, led to the prevailing style of carving we see today. At first, artists tried using chicken, turkey, and pheasant feathers in place of traditional hawk, eagle, and owl plumage, but the general consensus was that these alternatives were poor substitutes and did not look right. Concluding that pattern, color, and proper scale were more important than texture, an increasing number of doll makers opted to carve and paint the feathers themselves.

It was only natural that, having achieved satisfactory results by making feathers part of the carving, doll makers would rise to the challenge of carving other katsina paraphernalia such as fabric, yarn, fur, bells, and shells. Today, the finest katsina dolls are complex, lifelike, and highly detailed examples, each carved primarily from a single piece of wood. Realism, action, and one-piece carving became the most important aesthetic criteria by which non-Hopi judge dolls. The more artistically carved tithu became the most highly prized by serious collectors.

In the 1970s, carvers began to develop a new style, which came to be known as "katsina sculpture." With these figures, the sculptor focuses attention on the katsina's head and, to a lesser extent, the torso. (FIG. 10) Legs disappear under a flowing shawl, and in only a few cases can feet be glimpsed. (FIG. 11) On this type of work, smoothness of finish becomes as important as detailing.

Occasionally, carvers will produce dolls that depict neither katsinam nor clowns. (FIG. 12) Village priests are among the more common non-katsina figures to be carved.

FIG. 10 (opposite, left): *Angaktsina (Long-hair katsina) and Angaktsinmana (Long-hair katsina maiden) sculpture by Lawrence Acadiz (courtesy Grey Dog Trading Co.).*

FIG. 11 (opposite, right): *Tuma'öykatsina (Kaolin Chin katsina) and Koyemsi ("Mudhead") sculpture by Wilmer Kaye. This katsina is named for the white clay (kaolin) that Hopi carvers formerly used (and occasionally still do) to prime their katsina dolls before painting them. He is a very old katsina who appeared at plaza dances but is rarely seen today (courtesy Grey Dog Trading Co.).*

FIG. 12:

Hómiitsi or "Homichi" (Field Mouse) by Kerry David. One of the most commonly seen dolls that has no religious context. This carving is based on the Hopi folktale about the mouse who defeated the prairie falcon or chicken hawk. At some point, someone clearly wanted a doll based on the story, and Field Mouse continues to be produced today (courtesy private collection).

A few carvers are reviving the traditional tithu style that prevailed
prior to World War II. (FIG. 13)
Many of these artists also use
original mineral and vegetal pigments exclusively. Others use
muted commercial paints to evoke
the feeling of faded and worn dolls.

Some traditionalists (Hopi and
non-Hopi alike) argue that contemporary Hopi katsina dolls, while
they may be works of art, are not
necessarily true tithu. Yet it can also
be argued that these katsina dolls
are the product of carvers who have
deeply held spiritual beliefs. In fact,
many carvers will avoid making certain tithu because they believe them
to be taboo. There are oft-told
tales of artists who cut themselves
severely when they attempted to
carve such a doll. Many Hopi also
argue that it is inappropriate and
illegitimate for women to carve katsina dolls and believe that those who
attempt to do so will come to harm.

FIG. 13:

*Sakwaho′te (Blue
Hoote) by Clark
Tenakhongva. He
appears at many
dances, sometimes
as an uncle to the
other katsinam
(courtesy Georgianna
Kennedy).*

Katsina dolls serve as a means by which outsiders may
better understand and appreciate Hopi culture and spiritual
values. This is especially true now that the general public
is respectfully excluded from observing most katsina ceremonies. Indeed, Hopi artists strive to create highly realistic
and lifelike renditions of katsinam so that collectors may
honor an aspect of Hopi culture that they would otherwise
not have an opportunity to experience first hand.

Chapter 2

Ceremonies for Life

*H*opi ceremonial life involves a complex group of activities that run throughout the year. Each Hopi village celebrates the katsina season on a different time schedule, with different clans and societies involved in specific dances. Certain katsinam appear in virtually every village while others may appear on only one or two of the three Hopi mesas. Many katsinam have variants, and not all variants appear in every village. There are more than three hundred different katsinam in the Hopi pantheon.

Ceremonial katsina societies generally sponsor the major dances. These societies consist of members from several different clans, and individual clans have authority to conduct specific rituals. Over the years, as certain Hopi clans have dissolved or merged with others, the katsina societies have assumed responsibility for those ceremonies that might otherwise have disappeared with their respective clans. The kikmongwi, or village headman, originally granted land to clans on the basis of their ability to perform rites or services vital to that village. For example, the badger clan provides healing roots and herbs, while the tobacco clan provides sacred tobacco.

The Hopi ceremonial year usually begins in November at Wuwtsim or Wuutsimwimi. This is when the ritual cycle is

FIG. 14: *Soyalkatsina (Solstice katsina) by Ros George (courtesy Grey Dog Trading Co.).*

determined for the year, and secret rites are performed. Only those who have been initiated into one of the men's societies, and are thus considered adults, may participate.

Late December or early January sees the katsinam return. On Third Mesa, the Soyalkatsina, or Solstice katsina, heralds this advent ceremony. He proceeds haltingly through the village, singing quietly, and blessing certain sacred places. (FIG. 14) The Soyalwimi or Soyalangwmi (Solstice ceremony) itself occurs shortly thereafter on all three mesas. The majority of the rituals are conducted in the village kivas, underground ceremonial chambers. Katsinam who appear include the Mastopkatsina, or Death Fly katsina, who performs symbolic fertilization of the women he encounters on Third Mesa. (FIG. 15) The kivas are also ritually opened by different katsinam at different villages. Soyalwimi— a time of fasting, reflection, and prayer—establishes the spiritual path for the coming year.

FIG. 15: *Mastopkatsina (Death Fly katsina) by Cecil Calnimptewa (courtesy private collection).*

FIG. 16: *Deer dancer by Laurence Dallas (courtesy Grey Dog Trading Co.).*

In January, few katsinam appear. Instead, social dances are held. Dancers costumed as buffalo and other game animals, especially those, like Deer Dancer, that live in the snowy mountains, help to ensure an abundant supply of game and bring snow sufficient to produce a successful harvest later in the year. (FIG. 16)

Powamuya, or Bean Dance, is observed in February and is primarily designed to foster crop germination and spiritual growth. In one of the most complex ceremonies, the katsinam emerge from the kivas with bean sprouts and small corn stalks, which they give to women and children. The miraculous appearance of beans and corn in the dead of winter foreshadows a bountiful summer harvest.

Many kiva ceremonies take place at this time. On First and Second mesas, Ahöla or Ahölwutaqa appears at dawn to open the kivas for the first day of Powamuya. (FIG. 17) The next day, he also helps distribute the crops to sacred places in the village. A Mongkatsina or chief katsina, Ahöla is a leader of great wisdom. Ewtoto is another Mongkatsina and also a katsina father who is knowledgeable about all katsina rituals. (FIG. 18) During Powamuya and on other ceremonial occasions, he performs village blessings to help bring clouds and rain.

FIG. 17: *Ahöla or Ahölwutaqa (a chief katsina) by Ros George (courtesy Grey Dog Trading Co.).*

FIG. 18: *Ewtoto (a chief katsina) by Alvin Navasie (courtesy private collection).*

FIG. 19: *Angwusnasomtaqa (Crow Mother katsina) by Jonathan Day (courtesy private collection).*

FIG. 20:

Angwushahay'i (Crow "Bride" or Woman katsina) by Ros George (courtesy Grey Dog Trading Co.).

Angwusnasomtaqa (FIG. 19) and Angwushahay'i (FIG. 20) are two versions of the same katsina who appears during Powamuya. In some villages, Angwusnasomtaqa is the Crow Mother and a katsina mother. She plays a pivotal role in the rites by which Hopi children are initiated into the katsina culture. She usually is portrayed carrying yucca whips. Angwushahay'i appears as the Crow "Bride" or Crow Woman on some mesas. Rising with the dawn, she proceeds throughout the village singing and carrying a tray of corn plants, which she distributes to the women of the village. On Third Mesa, the roles of these two figures are reversed. Some Hopi consider these figures to represent two aspects of one being. Others say, "They are the same...but different."

On Second Mesa, Qöötsav or the Ashes katsina arrives to purify everything and everyone before the large Powamuya procession begins. (FIG. 21) A favorite katsina of mine is the Wuyaqqötö, known as Broad Face or Big Head. (FIG. 22) He is a yucca whip-wielding enforcer who is responsible for ensuring that spectators honor the sacred nature of the proceedings and make way for the colorful Powamuya procession.

Unfortunately, when tourists are present, the role of Wuyaqqötö often becomes more real than symbolic. Many outsiders forget that they are guests of the Hopi and behave crassly, as though katsina

FIG. 21: *Qöötsav (Ashes katsina) by Cecil Calnimptewa (courtesy private collection).*

dances are simply colorful shows staged for the amusement of visitors rather than sacred, celebratory rituals. Wuyaqqötö, the guard, has been known to force some of the more disruptive outsiders into compliance. Guests who are privileged to observe katsina rituals are strictly prohibited from taking photos or recordings of any kind. Violators have had their camera and recording equipment confiscated, and in some cases destroyed.

"I want more people to experience dances so they can appreciate Hopi religion and tradition," carver Alfred "Bo" Lomahquahu told me once, and I know many other Hopi share this view. However, because of the thoughtlessness of a few, many katsina ceremonies once open to the public are now off-limits.

FIG. 23:

Kwikwilyaqa (Mocking katsina) by Brian Honyouti (courtesy private collection).

FIG. 22: *Wuyaqqötö (Broad Face or Big Head katsina) by Kevin Pochoema (courtesy private collection).*

Kwikwilyaqa, the Mocking or Imitator katsina, is a comical figure in the Powamuya procession. (FIG. 23) He imitates and exaggerates the behavior of other katsinam and spectators alike. If he sees an onlooker scratching, he scratches himself. If a person crosses his or her arms, he does too. Kwikwilyaqa will pester his hapless victim until someone else catches his attention. Eventually, he shifts his attention to the other katsinam, who will become so annoyed that they conspire to get rid of him. One of the conspirators will pretend to set fire to his own hair. The Kwikwilyaqa mimics this, and "accidentally" sets his bark hair aflame. The other katsinam and spectators get the last laugh.

The Powamuya procession is perhaps the most impressive of the year because so many different katsinam appear. Talavaykatsina, the Dawn or Morning katsina (FIG. 24), often bestows presents at dawn along with several other katsinam. Huuhuwa, the Cross-legged katsina (FIG. 25), is another gift-giver. He embodies the spirit of a kind, crippled man who was especially good and generous in life. The Nangöysohut, Chasing Star or Morning and Evening Stars, are recognized by their distinctive, plains-style headdresses and always appear in pairs, just as the Morning Star "chases" the Evening Star across the sky. (FIG. 26)

Another important event at Powamuya is the coming of the Soo′so′yokt, or Ogre katsinam. So′yokwùuti, or Ogre Woman, appears first, visiting every home and demanding that the girls prepare complicated sacred foods and that the boys hunt for large game. (FIG. 27) If the food is not ready by the time she returns, she will threaten to take

FIG. 25:

Huuhuwa (Cross-legged katsina) by Robert Albert (courtesy Grey Dog Trading Co.).

FIG. 24:

Talavaykatsina (Dawn or Morning katsina) by Henry Naha (courtesy private collection).

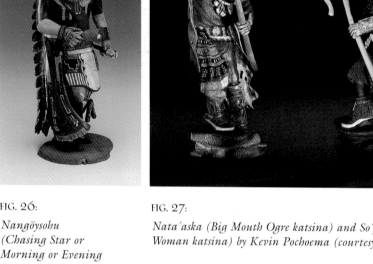

FIG. 26:

Nangöysohu (Chasing Star or Morning or Evening Star katsina) by Brendan Kay-quoptewa (courtesy private collection).

FIG. 27:

Nata'aska (Big Mouth Ogre katsina) and So'yokwùuti (Ogre Woman katsina) by Kevin Pochoema (courtesy private collection).

the children away and eat *them* instead. A few days later, she comes back with other ogres, including the Big Mouth Ogre or Ogre Uncle, called Nata'aska on First and Second mesas. (FIG. 27) The Wiharu, or White Ogre, may also appear. (FIG. 28) So'yokwùuti makes her demands for tribute over a ferocious din of background noise. Inevitably, she rejects the food offerings as insufficient and the members of each household are berated for their spiritual and secular failings in life.

Only when they receive what they deign to be sufficient booty do they leave. Having collected great quantities of food, the Soo'so'yokt are next drawn into a dance. The men of the village, acting together, interrupt the revelry and forcefully drive off the Ogres without their prizes. This ritual underscores what the Hopi people think about such qahopi, or outrageous, non-Hopi behavior and how the Hopi deal with greedy, exploitive, and bullying characters.

The Patsavu ceremony is incorporated into Powamuya during years in which adulthood initiations have been conducted during the preceding November Wuwtsim. Hee´e´e, the Warrior Maiden and a mother katsina, is a major figure at Patsavu. (FIG. 29) She leads the katsina procession and helps ensure that the secrecy of this sacred rite is strictly enforced. She is portrayed with half of her long, black hair up in a maiden's whorl and half loose and flowing. One legend has it that Hee´e´e was having her hair "put up" when she learned her village was being attacked while the men were away. She immediately jumped up and ran to lead the other women in defending the village until the men could return and help drive off the marauders.

The Angk´wa (literally translated as "after") are night dances that generally take place in the kivas in March, following Powamuya. These celebrations help promote crop germination and bring blessings to the Hopi. Gifts of food are presented to the spectators to signify the bounty of that year's harvest. Each kiva sponsors a separate dance. It is an amazing sight to see the various groups of katsinam making

FIG. 28: *Wiharu (White Ogre) by Orin Poley (courtesy private collection).*

FIG. 29: *Hee´e´e (Warrior katsina maiden) by Rick James (courtesy Grey Dog Trading Co.).*

their rounds during the course of the evening, visiting each kiva in turn until well past midnight. At each kiva, they announce their presence and are invited to enter. One by one, the katsinam climb down the ladder into the sacred chamber, where they proceed to dance and sing, their wonderfully rich baritone song echoing through the village. Then they depart back up the ladder and into the night, to be followed by the next group of katsinam.

One of the Angk'wa rituals is the Paalölöqangwu, or Water Serpent ceremony, which is only held in certain villages. This rite is performed to ensure an abundant harvest. The Hahay'i or Hahay'iwuuti (FIG. 2) is likely

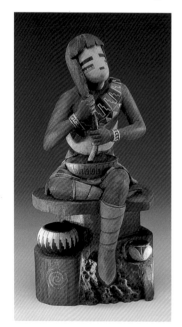

to appear at this time, but she also may play a role in other ceremonies such as Powamuya, accompanying the Ogres, and Patsavu, as a gift giver. The Hanomana, known as Tewa or Hano Maiden, also may appear at the Paalölöqangwu. (FIG. 30) Like the Hahay'iwùuti tithu, the Hanomana doll is one of the first given to young children, especially those in Hanoki or Tewa Village.

Kokopölö, the Humpbacked or Robber Fly katsina, is a fertility figure for plants and people who also appears during Angk'wa. (FIG. 31)) Because of his stooped posture and similar-sounding name, Kokopölö is sometimes mistaken for the ubiquitous Kokopelli, the

FIG. 30:

Hanomana (Tewa or Hano katsina maiden) by Alfred "Bo" Lomahquahu (courtesy private collection).

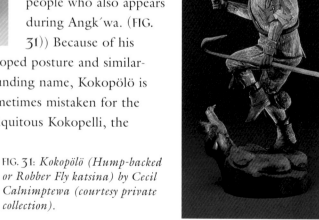

FIG. 31: *Kokopölö (Hump-backed or Robber Fly katsina) by Cecil Calnimptewa (courtesy private collection).*

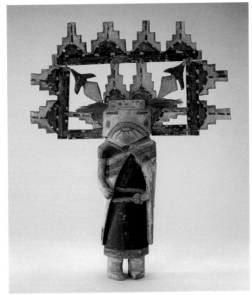

FIG. 32: *Poliikatsina*
(Butterfly katsina)
by Ronald Honyouti
(courtesy private collection).

FIG. 33: *Poliimana (Butterfly katsina maiden)*
or Palhikwmana (a Corn-grinding maiden),
artist unknown, circa 1890 (courtesy private
collection).

Hump-backed Flute Player whose visage is found on
prehistoric pottery, rock art, and contemporary works.
Kokopölö, however, seldom appears with a flute and his
"hump" is full of seeds.

Poliikatsina, the Butterfly katsina, and Poliimana, the
Butterfly katsina maiden (FIGS. 32 and 33), perform at the
Angk'wa night dances on Third Mesa. The latter, sometimes called Palhikwmana or Corn-grinding Maiden, also
performs with the Leenangwkatsina, or Flute katsina,
(FIG. 6) and a clown chorus. As with Angwusnasomtaqa
and Angwushahay'i, there is the sense that the Poliimana
and Palhikwmana maidens are two parts of the same being.

Daytime plaza dances, many of which are sponsored by
the women, occur periodically from March through June.
These dances are seen as prayers to promote crop growth
and a successful harvest. The katsinam usually distribute

gifts of food and other tokens, and receive sacred food offerings from the village women, in return. Feasts are usually held in conjunction with these rites and, if the dance was especially well received, the sponsors may ask the katsinam to return the following day.

Qötsahònkatsina, or White Bear katsina, participates in the plaza dances and is considered to have curative powers. (FIG. 34) Other animal katsinam who may appear include the Sowi'ingwkatsina, or Deer katsina (FIG. 35), Tsöpkatsina or Tsivkatsina, the Antelope katsina, and Kwewu or Kwèwkatsina, the Wolf katsina (FIG. 9). Sowi'ingw-katsina and Tsöpkatsina dance together while the predator Kwèwkatsina stalks them. The

FIG. 35:

Sowi'ingwkatsina (Deer katsina) by Brian Honyouti (courtesy private collection).

FIG. 34: *Qötsahònkatsina (White Bear katsina) by Ronald Honyouti (courtesy Grey Dog Trading Co.).*

game animal katsinam hold long sticks, which represent their forelegs, and dance to bring rain necessary for good forage. The Kwèwkatsina carries a staff that represents a tree, behind which he can hide and peer furtively at his prey: Deer and Antelope. This rite helps promote abundant, well-fed game and successful hunts. Pangkatsina or Pàngwkatsina, the Mountain Sheep or Ram katsina, also appears in plaza dances to promote spring rainfall. (FIG. 36) Kawàykatsina, or Horse katsina, promotes the health and expansion of the herd. (FIG. 37) Wakaskatsina, the Cow katsina, is a relatively new katsina who supports domestic livestock and honors the sacrifice they make to help feed the Hopi. (FIG. 38)

FIG. 37: *Kawàykatsina (Horse katsina) by Cecil Miles (courtesy Grey Dog Trading Co.).*

Tuhavi, the Paralyzed katsina, typically is carried on the shoulders of a blind Koyemsi or Kooyemsi, the katsina commonly known as the "Mudhead." (FIG. 39) According to legend, the two found themselves alone together after their village was attacked and destroyed. Individually, they were doomed. But working together, they were able to hunt for food and survive in the wilderness. Tuhavi became Koyemsi's "eyes," while able-bodied Koyemsi became Tuhavi's "legs." Eventually they were reunited with their neighbors and were venerated for their heroic example of mutual dependence and cooperative action.

Some katsinam who appear at these plaza dances represent the spirits of other tribes. The Tasapkatsina or Tasavkatsina, the Navajo katsina

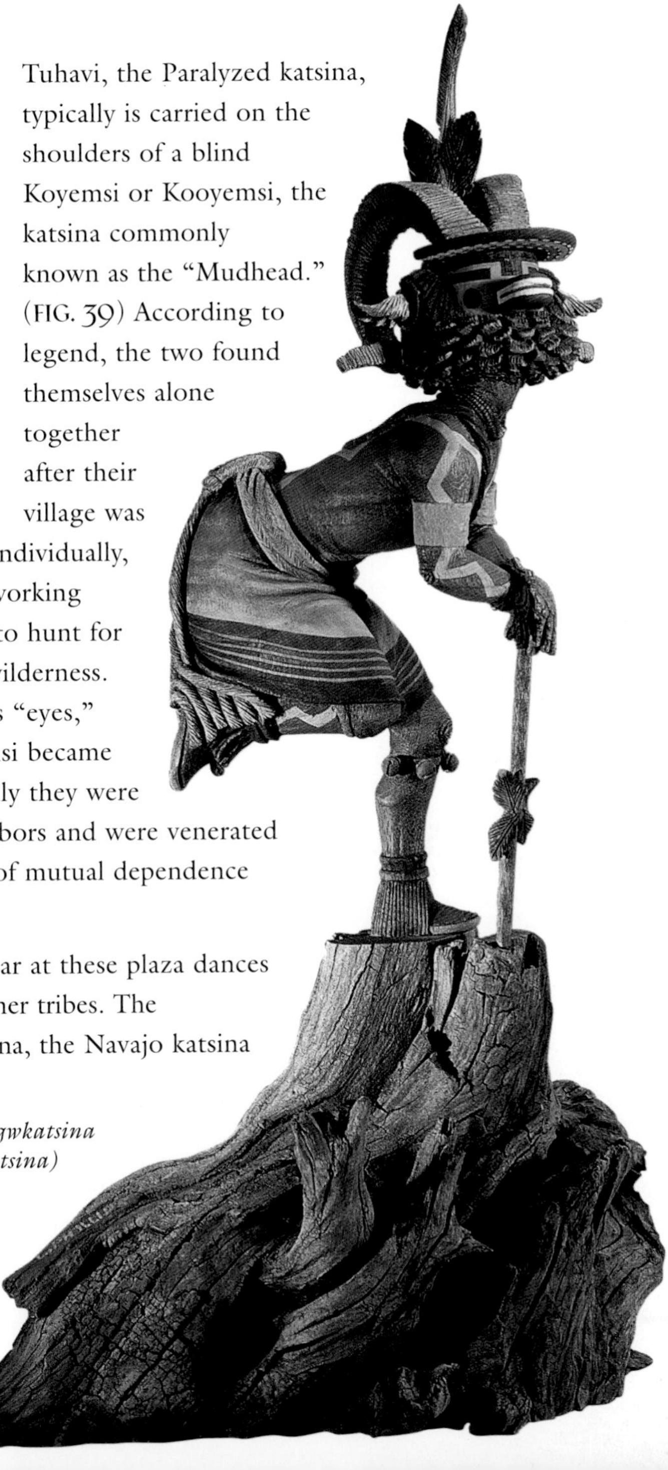

FIG. 36: *Pangkatsina or Pàngwkatsina (Ram or Mountain Sheep katsina) by Loren Phillips (courtesy private collection).*

(FIG. 4), often accompanies Yé'ii Bicheii or Yeyvitsha, the Navajo Grandfather katsina (FIG. 40), who pantomimes the message of the katsinam song. Other tribal spirits include Komantsi, the Comanche katsina (FIG. 41), Yotsi'-katsina, the Apache katsina (frontispiece), and Si'oktsina, the Zuni katsina.

Angaktsina or Long-hair katsina has many variants. (FIG. 10) While all katsinam help bring rain, Angak-tsina and the maidens who appear with him in the plaza dances are especially instru-mental in conveying this blessing. Angak-tsinmana, the Long-hair Maiden, and Takurmana, the Yellow Corn Maiden, are two of these rainmaking katsinas. (FIGS. 10 and 42) Angaktsina's long hair and beard sym-bolize rain, and the multicolored band on his face represents the rainbow.

FIG. 38 : *Wakaskatsina (Cow katsina) by Dennis Tewa (courtesy Grey Dog Trading Co.).*

Corn is one of the most important staples in the Hopi diet, and corn-meal is used to bless the katsinam and sacred places. Katsinam who specifically bless the corn harvest are Qa´ökatsina, the Corn katsina; Avatshoya, or Speckled Corn katsina,

FIG. 40 below: *Yé´ii Bicheii or Yeyvitsha (the Navajo Grandfather katsina) by Kevin Pochoema (courtesy Grey Dog Trading Co.).*

FIG. 39 above: *Tuhavi (Paralyzed katsina) and Koyemsi ("Mudhead") by Brian Laban (courtesy Grey Dog Trading Co.).*

FIG. 42: *Takurmana (Yellow Corn katsina maiden)*
by Jonathan Day (courtesy private collection).

FIG. 41: *Komantsi*
(Comanche katsina)
by Ronald Honyouti
(courtesy private
collection).

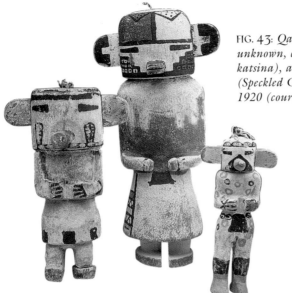

FIG. 43: *Qa'ökatsina (Corn katsina), artist unknown, circa 1890; Poos'humkatsina (Seed katsina), artist unknown, circa 1910; Avatshoya (Speckled Corn katsina), artist unknown, circa 1920 (courtesy private collection).*

FIG. 44: *Angwusi or Angwus-katsina (Crow katsina) by Loren Phillips (courtesy private collection).*

which represents the different colors of Hopi corn; and Poos'humkatsina, the Seed katsina, who brings the kernels for planting. (FIG. 43)

The Kipokkatsinam, or Warrior katsinam, play one of the most dramatic roles in the plaza dances. They include Angwusi or Angwuskatsina, the Crow; Tsorposyaqahöntaqa, sometimes called the "War Leader;" and Suyang'ephoya, the Left-handed katsina who is also a mighty hunter. (FIGS. 44, 45 and 46) Manang'yakatsina, the Lizard katsina, is another warrior who also represents beauty and is the intermediary to whom young men who desire a beautiful

FIG. 45:
Tsorposyaqahöntaqa ("War Leader"), artist unknown, circa 1920 (courtesy private collection).

FIG. 47:
Manang'yakatsina (Lizard Katsina), artist unknown, circa 1920 (courtesy private collection).

FIG. 46:
Suyang'ephoya (Left-handed katsina) by Kevin Pochoema (courtesy Grey Dog Trading Co.).

young wife may appeal. (FIG. 47) Mongwu, the Great Horned Owl katsina, is the warrior katsina best known for combating the clowns. (FIG. 48)

Koyaala, or Koshare, and Tsuku are the comically obnoxious adversaries of the Kipokkatsinam. (FIGS. 49 and 50) Gangs of Koyaalam or Tsutskut make their entrance by clambering over the rooftops and down into the plaza, and their wild behavior is irreverent, disruptive, disrespectful in the extreme...and hilarious. These clowns are not actually katsinam. However, they do enliven the plaza dances by serving as social critics or "wise fools," mocking the foibles of spectators, residents of neighboring Hopi villages, bureaucrats, authority figures, and outsiders alike. On one memorable occasion, a group of clowns skewered the medical profession by performing a mock operation behind a white sheet, pulling "organs" of raw meat out of an unfortunate patient and hurling them around the plaza. Of course, all of these jokesters either ignore or mock the admon-

FIG. 48: *Mongwu (Great Horned Owl katsina) by Ros George (courtesy Grey Dog Trading Co.).*

ishments of the Kipokkatsinam until the warriors reach a breaking point. Seizing the initiative, the Kipokkatsinam beat, strip, and douse the clowns until they repent and beg for mercy.

Other whimsical characters include Tasavu—a special clown who satirizes the perceived, stereotypical foibles of the Hopi's Navajo neighbors (FIG. 51)—and Koyemsi or Kooyemsi, the Mudhead katsina. (FIG. 52) When Koyemsi is not bearing Tuhavi, the Paralyzed katsina, he may appear as a dance leader, drummer, singer, or racer. He also assists the other katsinam and may distribute seeds and other gifts

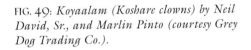

FIG. 50: *Tsuku (a clown) by Robert Albert (courtesy Grey Dog Trading Co.).*

FIG. 49: *Koyaalam (Koshare clowns) by Neil David, Sr., and Marlin Pinto (courtesy Grey Dog Trading Co.).*

FIG. 51: *Tasavu (Navajo clown) by Cecil Calnimptewa (courtesy private collection).*

and play games with spectators. The warrior version of Koyemsi, Kipokkoyemsi, joins with Mongwu and other Kipokkatsinam to battle the clowns. At least one carver has depicted him holding the moccasin of a defeated clown. (FIG. 53)

Wawarkatsinam, the Racer katsinam, test (and thereby promote) the health and endurance of male spectators by challenging them to footraces. Each kiva in the village sponsors its own race, so the events take place over several weeks. The contestants compete for prizes, often breads, but woe to the losers who face ritual public humiliation. Kokopölmana, the Hump-backed or

FIG. 52:

Koyemsi or Kooyemsi ("Mudhead") by Ronald Honyouti (courtesy private collection).

FIG. 53: *Kipokkoyemsi (Warrior or Attack "Mudhead") by Alred "Bo" Lomahquahu (courtesy Grey Dog Trading Co.).*

Robber Fly katsina maiden, will throw a laggard to
the ground and pretend to have sex with him, symboli-
cally promoting fertility. (FIG. 73) Tsilimoktaqa or
Tsilinonopnaqa, the Chili katsina, will stuff the loser's
mouth with hot chilies. (FIG. 54) Wiktsina, or Greasy katsina, will rub soot and grease all over his defeated oppo-
nent. (FIG. 55) I once saw two Wiktsinam set upon an
unfortunate Hopi who had fallen asleep during a ceremony:
By the time they were through, their victim was wide-
awake, and pitch black from head to foot. Sösö'pa or
Sösööpa, the Cricket katsina, will thrash a loser with yucca

FIG. 54: *Tsilinonopnaqa or Tsilimoktaqa (Chili Pepper katsina) by Stetson Hon-yumptewa (courtesy private collection).*

FIG. 55: *Wiktsina (Greasy katsina) by Ronald Honyouti (courtesy private collection).*

FIG. 56: *Sösö'pa or Sösööpa (Cricket katsina) by Clyde Honyouti (courtesy private collection).*

FIG. 58: *Katsinmana or Hemiskatsinmana (Katsina maiden or Hemiskatsina maiden) by Brian Laban (courtesy private collection).*

whips. (FIGS. 56 and 9) Once the losers have suffered their respective fates, all contestants receive blessing and gifts from the katsinam.

The Niman or Nimaniwu, commonly known as the Home Dance, occurs in July and marks the conclusion of the katsinam ceremonial cycle. The main figure in this dance is usually the Hemiskatsina, a Home Dance katsina, who typically is accompanied by Hemiskatsinmana, or katsina maiden. (FIGS. 57 and 58) Hohomana or Hoohòomana, the Zuni katsina maiden (FIG. 59), and Qötsamana or Nuvaktsinmana, the Snow katsina maiden, also may appear. Early in the day, the Hemiskatsinam present gifts tied to cornstalks, which represent success for the crops yet to come. Near the end of the cere-

FIG. 57: *Hemiskatsinam (a Home Dance katsinam) by Sam Kayquoptewa (courtesy Grey Dog Trading Co.).*

FIG. 60: *Ma'lo, artist unknown, circa 1930 (courtesy private collection).*

FIG. 59: *Hohomana or Hoohòomana (Zuni katsina maiden) by Ros George (courtesy Grey Dog Trading Co.).*

mony, brides also receive special blessings, gifts, and tithu. Sometimes, other katsinam appear as the Niman-katsina. These may include Angaktsina, the Long-hair katsina; Tasapkatsina, the Navajo katsina; and on rare occasions Ma'lo, an ancient rain katsina. (FIG. 60) After the final dance, the katsinam prepare to depart from the Hopi mesas, taking the prayers of the faithful with them. A ritual on the day after Niman ceremonially closes the cycle that started so many months ago.

On very rare occasions during Niman, the Sa'lako cere-mony is held. Sa'lakwtaqa, Sa'lako man (FIG. 67), and Sa'lakwmana, Sa'lako maiden, appear with Tukwunàngw-katsina, the Cumulus Cloud katsina (FIG. 72) and Tukwunangwmana, the Cumulus Cloud katsina maiden

FIG. 61: *Tukwunangwmana (Cumulus Cloud katsina maiden) by Ros George (courtesy private collection).*

FIG. 63: *Polimana (social Butterfly maiden dancer) by Kevin Pochoema (courtesy Robert Hart collection).*

(FIG. 61). These katsinam enact a ritual that conveys an especially fervent prayer for rain.

Màasaw is the only katsina who does not return to the spirit world after Niman. (FIG. 62) He remains with the Hopi always and may appear at any time. This is because he is more of a diety than a katsina. Màasaw bequeathed the Hopi lands to the Hopi people and gave them fire and the gift of agriculture in this, the Fourth World. Màasaw also safely shepherds the dead to Maski, the underworld or afterworld, where they are transformed into katsinam.

After the katsinam season concludes, August and September are filled with many ritual activities. The Snake—Antelope and Flute ceremonies occur on alternate years to entice the last of the rains to fall before harvest time. During the Snake—Antelope ceremony, members of the Snake clan dance with live snakes, including venomous rattlesnakes, clenched between their teeth. Social dances, including the Polìit or Butterfly dance that imparts blessings and thanks for a successful growing season, also take place during the fall. (FIG. 63) The ceremonial cycle concludes with a series of social dances sponsored by the Women's Societies.

FIG. 62: *Màasaw (Earth, Life, and Death deity), doll on left, artist unknown, circa 1930–40 (courtesy private collection); doll on right by Cecil Calnimptewa (courtesy Grey Dog Trading Co.).*

Chapter 3

The Art of Katsina Doll Carving

A well-carved katsina doll is easy to admire as a work of art, but the real spirit of a tihu is found within. Brian Laban, a noted carver from First Mesa, calls it "seeing through the outside of the wood."

Katsina dolls are traditionally carved from the roots of cottonwood trees. which once were abundant on and near the Hopi lands. (FIG. 64) The Hopi word for cottonwood root is paako, which means water wood, and the cottonwood root's ability to seek and find abundant water mirrors the ability of the katsinam to do the same for the Hopi people.

Robert Albert of Mùnqapi says one of the hardest parts about carving a katsina doll is "finding a good root. Part of Hopi spirituality is to collect it yourself." Today, carvers may travel hundreds of miles throughout the Southwest looking for this special material.

Some Hopi carvers purchase cottonwood roots from outsiders. Other carvers have resorted to using cottonwood branches, while still others have abandoned using cottonwood altogether in favor of a more abundant and easily obtainable material, such as tupelo, a swamp wood from the southeastern United States.

FIG. 64: *Cottonwood roots (courtesy Robert Albert).*

After finding a workable root, the carver must "cure" it by letting it dry completely. He also must be sure that it is relatively free of pockets of sand or hard knots, both of which can pose serious obstacles during carving. Only then can the artist begin to rough out the tihu. Some carvers insist on performing every painstaking step by hand and disdain "modern" power tools altogether. Other artists prefer to use a time saving band saw or a die grinder during the rough-out phase, and a belt sander to flatten the base of the figure. Carvers employ a wide assortment of knives and gouges during the initial carving stage, and keep many types of sharpening devices at hand to ensure that their tools remain well honed. The best artists seem to spend as much time sanding a katsina doll with fine sandpaper as they do carving, but this extra effort makes a tremendous difference in the final piece. (FIG. 65)

The technique of katsina doll painting has changed dramatically since 1970. Earlier, most carvers typically used tempera paints. Artists credit Brian Honyouti, now of Hotvela, with initiating the use of wood preservatives and varnishes instead of paint on certain surfaces, especially the skin. By creating dramatic contrast between painted and unpainted areas, Honyouti introduced a new level of artistic expression to katsina dolls.

FIG. 65: *Katsina doll carving tools including sanding sticks, sharpening stones and leather strop, paint brushes, acrylic paints, assorted knives and gouges (courtesy Lawrence Acadiz).*

FIG. 66: *Motorized katsina doll carving tools: wood burning tool and rotary tool (courtesy Lawrence Acadiz).*

Today's finest carvers follow Honyouti's lead, generally in one of several ways. Some carvers apply linseed oil and oil-based paints, and create subtle color variations by mixing pigments with different concentrations of thinner. Linseed oil tends to dry slowly, so some artists may opt to use stains and oil-based or acrylic paints. Still others use spray wood sealers and acrylic paints that they often thin with water. A few carvers who specialize in creating old-style revival dolls eschew commercial paint altogether in favor of traditional mineral and vegetal paints. Experimentation seems to be the only rule, and one of the most exciting and rewarding aspects of katsina carving is discovering what materials and colors will work best in the final presentation.

Von Monongya is generally cited as the first to introduce and advocate the use of wood-burning tools. This technique is especially effective when detailing hair, feathers, and hands. Motorized rotary tools can achieve similar results. (FIG. 66) Carvers employ many methods to achieve the desired effects in their work. (FIG. 67)

D.

Most Hopi, artists and non-artists alike, strongly object to non-Pueblo carvers making katsina dolls. Imitation is not the sincerest form of flattery when the subject is katsina dolls. Tithu, even those carved for commercial sale, are representations of spiritual beings who are intimately associated with the life ways of the Hopi and other Pueblo peoples. While contemporary Christians may be happy to have traditional-looking Crèche figurines that were made by Buddhists in China, the Hopi believe it is extremely offensive

A.

B.

C.

FIG. 67:

Sa'lakwtaqa (Male Sa'lako katsina) by Lawrence Acadiz (courtesy Grey Dog Trading Co.):
A. roughed out
B. pre-detailing
C. nearly finished with initial painting
D. finished with tablita (wooden head piece) added.

and disrespectful for tithu to be produced by non-Pueblo peoples who are not grounded in Hopi spirituality.

The Hopi reserve their greatest contempt for cheap, mass-produced Navajo "knock offs" and craft shop kits. Almost all of these are made from multiple, machine-turned pine parts, with glued-on fur and feathers and even plastic clothing. (FIG. 68) The katsinam play no role in Navajo religion whatsoever. A Navajo "kachina doll carving," although "Indian made," is as non-traditional and unauthentic as a Taiwanese or Mexican "kachina doll carving" would be.

FIG. 68:

Navajo carving (courtesy private collection).

Some people argue that cheap "knock offs" offer people a more affordable alternative to authentic Hopi tithu. Discriminating buyers who appreciate what the katsinam represent will only purchase authentic Hopi katsina dolls. Indeed, real Hopi tithu are available in a wide range of prices, and fine works by younger Hopi artists who are new to carving are very reasonably priced.

What should buyers look for in a katsina doll? The best carvers pride themselves on precise attention to detail and proper proportioning of the body. They also strive to capture realistic, dramatic action. (FIG. 48) Hands are especially difficult to carve well. Accurately rendered hands, down to fingernails, with separated fingers rather than tightly closed fists, are the marks of a master carver. (FIG. 59)

Proportion is another criterion by which to judge the quality of a katsina doll. Many carvers make arms and legs that are too long or short relative to the body of the doll. Heads are often too small and feet may seem overly large. Details in hair, feathers, paraphernalia, and jewelry should be as finely done as possible. If the figure is striking a dramatic pose, are the hair, feathers, clothing, and necklaces moving with it? (FIG. 46) A very adept artist will separate clothing, limbs, and held objects from the body. (FIG. 44)

It is much more difficult to render a cloak flapping out and away in the breeze than one which is simply and statically draped against the body.

Ideally, a katsina doll should be carved almost entirely from a single piece of wood. No one knows precisely when, or by whom, the first "one-piece" tihu showing motion was carved, but we do know that such dolls were available for sale as early as the 1950s. Brian Honyouti claims his father Clyde was one of the earliest such carvers. The elder Honyouti was a shepherd who carved while watching over his flock. Under the circumstances, he found it easier to carry and work on a single, large cottonwood root rather than deal with several smaller pieces.

"One-piece" carving is something of a misnomer. Carvers often add "hand-held" objects, feathers on top of the head, yarn ties and leg bells, "goggle eyes," and bases. Some carvers still add limbs. This is particularly acceptable on bird katsina dolls that have outstretched wings. A few artists prefer to carve heads separately. Carvings to which basic body parts have been added as a matter of convenience or expedience should not command the highest prices. Carefully look for telltale signs, such as dried glue spots around the neck or join spots, to see how many elements may have been added. A reputable dealer will be able to point out what has been added. A true one-piece doll is a valuable find. (FIGS. 69, 20, and 38)

FIG. 69:

Iyoho'wùuti or Masanwùuti (Cold-bringing or Gesture Woman katsina) by Ed Tewanema. She helps bring snow in the winter for summer crops. During Powamuya she messes up people's hair to illustrate what winter storms do (courtesy Grey Dog Trading Co.).

FIG. 70: *Tsutskut (clowns, plural of Tsuku) by Robert Albert (courtesy Grey Dog Trading Co.).*

FIG. 71: *To'tsa or Tòotsa (Hummingbird katsina) by Brendan Kayquoptewa. Appearing in night or plaza dances, the Hummingbird helps plants bloom (courtesy private collection).*

Carving more than one figure on a single base is extremely difficult. While multiple figure work has been around for decades, artists have only recently stepped up to the supreme challenge of carving multiple katsinam from one piece of wood. (FIG. 70)

Fine sanding, which leads to a smooth finish, is a critical mark of a quality doll (frontispiece), as is accurate painting. Many good carvers may not be especially good painters, but the best artists have mastered both skills. Look for straight or properly curved lines and even coverage of details, unless the artist purposely thinned his paints to achieve less opacity and let the character of the wood show through.

Recently, more ambitious artists have begun to carve elaborate bases for their katsina dolls, spending days, if not weeks, on these alone. These bases often incorporate details and associated symbols that relate to the particular katsina. (FIG. 71) Sometimes they set the katsina into an all-encompassing theme involving the katsina's function. (FIG. 72) The scenes may not necessarily have a specific religious content. Brian Honyouti not only creates interesting bases, but often does work on their bottoms as well. (FIGS. 23, 73, 74, and 75)

When I started collecting katsina dolls in the 1950s and 60s, I could purchase an average tihu for as little as $8 and no more than $25. Of course, the amount of time it took to create those dolls was nowhere near what today's carvers invest in their work. A medium to large katsina doll created by a master carver may retail for $2,000 or considerably more. Even good miniatures will be fairly priced at $500. Less refined pieces can start around $100. Artists who win awards at major Native American art shows generally can command higher prices for their work.

Some buyers prefer the look and character of older, pre-war dolls. Unfortunately, authentic old dolls are exceedingly rare. Most examples

FIG. 72: *Tukwunàngwkatsina (Cumulus Cloud katsina) by Alfred "Bo" Lomahquahu (courtesy private collection).*

of this type that I see on the market are either fakes or have been heavily restored or repainted and thus have little collectible value. In order to evaluate a doll's authenticity, one needs to have a good knowledge of paints used during different time periods and must be able recognize logical wear patterns. I would encourage anyone who is seriously interested in collecting old dolls to first study dolls that have been authenticated, and to consult with an experienced dealer who can point out signs of restoration or fakery.

FIG. 75: *The base of the Mongwuwùuti showing the Owl's eye (courtesy Grey Dog Trading Co.).*

FIG. 73: *Kokopölmana (Hump-backed or Robber Fly katsina maiden) by Brian Honyouti. This is the base of the Kwikwilyaqa in* FIG. 23 *(courtesy private collection).*

FIG. 74:
Mongwuwùuti (Great Horned Owl katsina woman) by Brian Honyouti. A katsina that is rarely seen, she may appear at night dances with Owl children (courtesy Grey Dog Trading Co.).

The most significant factor to consider when deciding whether to buy a katsina doll is how well you like the piece. If it is well executed but its soul doesn't speak to you, you shouldn't buy it. And don't buy a doll simply for its perceived investment value. Fine work tends to appreciate in value over time, but that should be looked upon as a nice bonus, not a reason to purchase. Different people look for different qualities in a doll, and tastes change. Some collectors like dramatic action dolls, some prefer dolls in a more traditional style, and some enjoy sculptures.

Like their fellow artists who work in other media, Hopi katsina carvers are a fascinating lot. Some speak eloquently about their work, while others are more reticent.

"I enjoy the challenge of carving and the patience and discipline it demands," says Ros George of Mùnqapi. "I want to continue to discover the artist within myself and really enjoy the learning process because there are always strengths to admire in someone else's creation."

Paaqavi carver Kevin Pochoema says, simply, "I keep trying to improve so I won't carve 'just another doll.'"

Respected carver and religious leader Dennis Tewa of Mùnqapi speaks for many of his fellow artists when he talks about the need to balance personal artistic expression with the communal values and traditions of Hopi culture.

"When I started carving, I wanted to carve every katsina to help preserve the Hopi religion," Tewa says. "Now I've learned to take my time in carving because there are so many creative, fine artists working today. I think Hopi young people now have less understanding of their heritage and are losing their language. This will not allow them to prepare for ceremonies properly, and if the katsinam stop coming it will be the end of Hopi culture."

These concerns are shared by the younger generation of carvers, particularly those who, like Lawrence Acadiz, live and work off the Hopi reservation.

"My work keeps me tied to Hopi culture," Acadiz explains. "It's a way to hold on to Hopi beliefs. I feel obligated to carve to be a part of it."

The love that these artists have for their community and their traditions shines through in the wonderfully expressive katsina dolls they create. All of the truly gifted carvers I have been fortunate to know bring a special feeling to their dolls. Whether it is their attention to ceremonial detail, an especially creative way of capturing a katsina's movement, or a natural sense of humor, there is something unique in each of these artists' creations.

Given the remarkable transformation in the art of katsina doll carving that occurred in the twentieth century, many people may wonder where the art form might be headed in the twenty-first. Trader Bruce McGee believes future katsina doll collectors may be more interested in a doll as fine art rather than as culturally inspired art. Buyers should take the time to study and appreciate the religious traditions on which these carvings are based. Only then can the katsinam truly speak to you.

Glossary

Ahöla or *Ahölwutaqa*—a chief katsina, 17

Angaktsina—Long-hair katsina, 10

Angaktsinmana—Long-hair katsina maiden, 10

Angk'wa—katsina night dances held after Powamuya, usually in March, 23

Angwushahay'i—Crow "Bride" or Woman katsina (Crow Mother katsina on Third Mesa), 18

Angwusnasomtaqa—Crow Mother katsina (Crow "Bride" or Woman katsina on Third Mesa), 18

Angwusi or *Angwuskatsina*—Crow katsina, 31

Avatshoya—Speckled Corn katsina, 31

Awat'ovi—a Hopi village that was destroyed in 1700, 2

Ewtoto—a father and chief katsina, 18

Hahay'i, Hahay'imana, or *Hahay'iwùuti*—a katsina mother, 6

Hanoki—Hano or Tewa Village, a First Mesa village that is mostly Tewa speaking, 1

Hanomana—Hano or Tewa katsina maiden, 24

Hee'e'e—Warrior katsina maiden and a mother katsina, 23

Hemiskatsina—leading katsina at Niman in some villages, 36

Hemiskatsinam—plural of Hemiskatsina, vii, 36

Hemiskatsinmana—Hemiskatsina maiden, 36

Hohomana or *Hoohòomana*—Zuni katsina maiden, 37

Hómiitsi or *"Homichi"*—Field Mouse from the Hopi folktale who fights the prairie falcon or chicken hawk, 12

Honànkatsina—Badger katsina, 9

Hotvela—Hotevilla, A Third Mesa village, 1

Huuhuwa—Cross-legged katsina, 21

Iyoho'wùuti—Cold-bringing Woman katsina (see *Masanwùuti*), 43

katsina—a spirit being, v

katsinam—plural of katsina, v

katsinmamant—plural of katsinmana, vii

katsinmana—a katsina maiden, vii

Katsinmana—katsina maiden that may appear with several different katsinam including the Hemiskatsina, 36

Kawàykatsina—Horse katsina, 27

kikmongwi—a village "chief," 15

kipokkatsinam—warrior or attacking katsinam, 31

Kipokkoyemsi—Warrior or Attack Koyemsi, 34, 46

Kiqötsmovi—Kykotsmovi or New Oraibi, a Third Mesa Village, 1 *kiva*—underground ceremonial chamber, 16

Kokopölmana—Hump-backed or Robber Fly katsina maiden, 34

Kokopölö— Hump-backed or Robber Fly katsina, 24

Komantsi—Comanche katsina, 30

Kooyemsi or *Koyemsi*—a figure who performs comical as well as more serious functions, often called the "Mudhead," 10, 29, 34

Koshare or *Koshari*—another name for Koyaala, 33

Koyaala—a New Mexican Pueblo-derived ceremonial clown, 33

Koyaalam—plural of Koyaala, 33

Koyemsim—plural of Koyemsi, 34

Kwèwkatsina or *Kwewu*—Wolf katsina, 9

Kwikwilyaqa—Mocking or Imitator katsina, 20

Kyarkatsina or *Kyaro*—Parrot katsina, 8

Leenangwkatsina or *Lenang-katsina*—Flute katsina, 8

Màasaw—a deity with power over land, fire, crops, death, and the underworld, 38

Ma'lo—a rarely seen old katsina that is rain related, 37

Manang'yakatsina—Lizard katsina, 32

Masanwùuti—Gesture Woman katsina (see *Iyoho'wùuti*), 43

Maski—Hopi underworld or after-world, 5, 8

Mastopkatsina—Death Fly katsina (a Third Mesa fertility katsina), 16

Mongkatsina—a chief katsina, 17

Mongwu—Great Horned Owl katsina, 32

Mongwuwùuti—Great Horned Owl katsina maiden, 46, 47

Mùnqapi—Moencopi, a Hopi village near Tuba city, 1

Musangnuvi—Mishongnovi, a Second Mesa village, 1

Muuyawkatsina—Moon katsina, 7

Naavuktsina—Prickly Pear (nopal) katsina, 8

Nangöysohu—a single Nangöysohut

Nangöysohut—Morning and Evening Star katsina pair, also called the Chasing Star katsinam (the morning and evening stars "chase" themselves across the skies), 22

Nata'aska—Big Mouth or "Black" Ogre katsina and an uncle katsina, 22

Niman or *Nimaniwu*—Home Dance held in July, vii, 36

Nimankatsina—a katsina appearing at the Home Dance, vii

Nuvaktsinmana—Snow katsina maiden (see *Qötsamana*), 36

Orayvi—Oraibi, a Third Mesa village, 1

paako—dried cottonwood root, 39

Paalölöqangkatsina—Water Serpent katsina, 7

Paalölöqangwu—Water Serpent ceremony, 7, 24

Paaqavi—Bacavi, a Third Mesa village, 1

Palhikwmana—a Corn-grinding katsina maiden (see *Polìimana*), 25

Tòotsa or *To'tsa*—Hummingbird katsina, 44

Tsilinonopnaqa or *Tsilimoktaqa*—Chili Pepper katsina, 35

Tsivkatsina or *Tsöpkatsina*—Antelope katsina, 26

Tsorposyaqahöntaqa—"War Leader" katsina, 32

Tsuku—a ceremonial clown, 33

Tsutskut—plural of Tsuku, 33, 34

Tuhavi—Paralyzed katsina, 29

Tukwunàngwkatsina—Cumulus Cloud katsina, 45

Tukwunangwmana—Cumulus Cloud katsina maiden, 37

Tuma'öykatsina—White Clay (or Kaolin) Chin katsina, 10

Waalpi—Walpi, a First Mesa village, 1

Wakaskatsina—Cow katsina, 28

Wawarkatsinam—Racer katsinam, 34

Wiktsina—Greasy katsina, 35

Wiharu—White Ogre katsina, 23

Wuutsimwimi or *Wuwtsim*—ceremony that sets the religious cycle for the year, 15

Wuyaqqötö—"Broad Face" or Big Head katsina, 20

Yé'ii Bicheii or *Yeyvitsha*—Navajo katsina grandfather, 29

Yotsi'katsina—Apache katsina, frontispiece

List of Carvers

Lawrence Acadiz: 6, 10, 41

Robert Albert: 21, 33, 44

Cecil Calnimptewa: Frontispiece, 16, 19, 24, 34, 38

Laurence Dallas: 17

Kerry David: 12

Neil David, Sr.: 33

Jonathan Day: 18, 30

Ros George: 16, 17, 18, 32, 37

Stetson Honyumptewa: 35

Brian Honyouti: 20, 26, 46, 47

Clyde Honyouti: 36

Ronald Honyouti: 25, 26, 30, 34, 35

Rick James: 23

Wilmer Kaye: 10

Brendan Kayquoptewa: 22, 44

Sam Kayquoptewa: 36

Brian Laban: 29, 36

Alfred "Bo" Lomahquahu: 24, 34, 45

Cecil Miles: 27

Henry Naha: 21

Alvin Navasie: 18

Loren Phillips: 27, 44

Marlin Pinto: 33

Kevin Pochoema: 20, 22, 29, 32, 38

Orin Poley: 23

Clark Tenakhongva: 13

Dennis Tewa: 28

Ed Tewanema: 43

Pronunciation Guide

'—a glottal stop between sounds as in unh-unh

a—ah as in w*a*tt

aa—same as ah in w*a*tt but more elongated

aw—ow as in c*ow*

ay—igh as in h*igh*

e—eh as in s*e*t

ee—same as eh in s*e*t but more elongated

ew—same as eh in s*e*t plus w (ehwuh)

h—h as in *h*ome

i—ee as in f*ee*t

ii—same as ee in f*ee*t but more elongated

iw—same as ee in f*ee*t plus w (eewuh)

iy—same as ee in f*ee*t plus y (eeyuh)

k—k as in s*k*ip

kw—qu as in s*qui*d

k'w—k, glottal stop, and w starting new syllable

ky—kew as in s*kew*

l—l as in *l*ike

m—m as in *m*ate

n—n as in *n*ame

ng—nasal ng as in lo*ng*

ngw—nasal ng and w run together, similar to la*ngu*age

ng'y—nasal ng, glottal stop, and y starting next syllable

o—o as in *o*mit

oo—same as o in *o*mit but more elongated

ö—German umlaut or French eu sound

öö—same as ö but more elongated

ow—ow as in fl*ow*

oy—oy as in t*oy*

öy—German umlaut or French eu plus y (öyuh)

p—p in s*p*in

q—guttural k

qw—guttural k and w run together

r—rsh as in ma*rsh* if found at the end of a syllable

s—s as in *s*it

t—t as in s*t*ill

ts—ts as in ba*ts*

u—oo as in w*oo*d

uu—same as oo in w*oo*d but more elongated

uw—ew as in fl*ew*

uy—oo as in w*oo*d plus y (ooyuh)

v—a weak v sound if found before a vowel or an f sound if found at the end of a syllable

w—w as in *w*on

y—y as in *y*our

á,é,í,ó,ú—vowels found in a stressed syllable

à,è,ì,ò,ù—vowels with a falling tone, especially in elongated vowels (àa, èe, ìi, òo, ùu) or in syllables with nasal sounds (àn, ùn)

Bibliography

Adams, E. Charles
1994 "The Katsina Cult: A Western Pueblo Perspective" in *Kachinas in the Pueblo World*. (Polly Schaafsma, ed.). Albuquerque: University of New Mexico Press.

Beaver, Bill
1992 "Collecting Kachina Dolls" in *Hopi Kachina Dolls* (*Plateau*, Vol. 63, No. 4). Flagstaff, AZ: Museum of Northern Arizona.

Brew, J. O.
1979 "Hopi Prehistory and History to 1850" in *Handbook Of North American Indians*, Vol. 9. (Alfonso Ortiz, ed.). Washington, DC: Smithsonian Institution.

Brody, J. J.
1994 "Kachina Images in American Art: The Way of The Doll" in *Kachinas in the Pueblo World*. (Polly Schaafsma, ed.). Albuquerque: University of New Mexico Press.

Connelly, John C.
1979 "Hopi Social Organization" in *Handbook Of North American Indians*, Vol. 9. (Alfonso Ortiz. ed.). Washington, DC: Smithsonian Institution.

Dockstader, Frederick M.
1979 "Hopi History, 1850–1940" in *Handbook of North American Indians*, Vol. 9. (Alfonso Ortiz, ed.).Washington, DC: Smithsonian Institution.

Erickson, Jon T.
1977 *Kachinas: An Evolving Hopi Art Form*. Phoenix: The Heard Museum.

Hieb, Louis A.
1979 "Hopi World View" in *Handbook Of North American Indians*, Vol. 9. (Alfonso Ortiz, ed.). Washington, DC: Smithsonian Institution.

1994 "The Meaning of Katsina: Toward a Cultural Definition of 'Person' in Hopi Religion" in *Kachinas in the Pueblo World*. (Polly Schaafsma, ed.). Albuquerque: University of New Mexico Press.

Hill, Kenneth C., et. al.

1998 *Hopi Dictionary/Hopìikwa Lavàytutuveni: A Hopi–English Dictionary of the Third Mesa Dialect*. Hopi Dictionary Project, Bureau of Applied Research in Anthropology, University of Arizona (Kenneth C. Hill, Emory Sekaquaptewa, Mary E. Black, and Ekkehart Malotki, eds.). Tucson: The University of Arizona Press.

Schaafsma, Polly

1994 "Introduction" in *Kachinas in the Pueblo World*. (Polly Schaafsma, ed.). Albuquerque: University of New Mexico Press.

Secakuku, Alph H.

1995 *Following the Sun and Moon: Hopi Kachina Tradition*. Flagstaff, AZ: Northland Publishing.

Teiwes, Helga

1991 *Kachina Dolls: The Art of Hopi Carvers*. Tucson: The University of Arizona Press.

Titiev, Mischa

1992 *Old Oraibi: A Study of the Hopi Indians of Third Mesa*. Albuquerque: University of New Mexico Press.

Wright, Barton

1973 *Kachinas: A Hopi Artist's Documentary Original Paintings by Cliff Bahnimptewa*. Flagstaff, AZ: Northland Press.

1977 *Hopi Kachinas: The Complete Guide to Collecting Kachina Dolls*. Flagstaff, AZ: Northland Press.

1994 *Clowns of The Hopi: Tradition Keepers and Delight Makers*. Flagstaff, AZ: Northland Publishing.

9-13-15

H2O A JOURNEY OF FAITH

PARTICIPANT'S GUIDE

The publishers want to thank Ross Brodfuehrer and Mike Mack for their collaboration and writing skills in developing the content for this book.

Published in Louisville, Kentucky by City on a Hill Studio.

City on a Hill Studio titles may be purchased in bulk for educational, business, fund-raising, or sales promotional use. For information please e-mail sales@cityonahillstudio.com

ISBN: 978-0-9829398-4-0

Contents

Welcome

Water. Our world couldn't exist without it. It covers our planet and fills our bodies. It keeps us alive. Jesus knew how important water was. Maybe that's why He called Himself the Living Water. He was making a claim and an offer too good to ignore. H2O is about water, the Living Water Jesus said He offered. If you're thirsty, you owe it to yourself to consider what He said . . . and who He is.

We are glad that you are taking part in H2O. We don't think you'll regret it.

The idea of these sessions is to explore Jesus, who He was and is, what He said, and what that means for you. There will be no heavy-handed preaching or manipulation. As a matter of fact, each group will abide by these principles:

Ground Rules

- Everyone is free to express his or her views, whether he or she is in agreement with the DVD message or not.

- No one is allowed to criticize or attack someone else's view, although you may express your own when it disagrees with someone else's.

- No one has to talk at all. You can simply sit and listen, if you prefer.

- Conversely, no one is allowed to talk all the time.

- We will start the dinner at _____o'clock and end each session by _____o'clock.

Welcome!

Each gathering will include a meal, a half-hour DVD presentation, and an open discussion. So, what's there to lose? Not much but some time out of your week. What is there to gain? At the very least, a deeper understanding of what others believe and why. At the most, if what Jesus says is true, a way to quench the deepest thirsts of your life.

This participant's guide will be your partner as you watch the seven compelling dramas in the H2O DVD series. The sessions outlined here will help you remember what you see and express how you feel about it. For each week you will see a section for Discussion and a section for Reflection. The Discussion section contains questions intended to guide the discussion for your group meeting. The Reflection section is for you to continue thinking and reflecting on your own throughout the week.

You're ready to get started. We hope you will enjoy this unique journey of discovery and faith.

LESSON 1

Thirsty

H20 INTRODUCTION

DISCUSSION

1. Kyle defined *thirst* as an inner desire that demands satisfaction and said that people are thirsty for something that can't be satisfied with the stuff of this world.

   ♪ What are your feelings about Kyle's statement?

§ If you feel people do experience that kind of deep thirst, how would you describe it?

§ If you don't think there is such a thirst, then how do you explain so many people feeling as though there is?

2. Oxford scholar C. S. Lewis was quoted in the presentation.

> Creatures are not born with desires unless satisfaction for those desires exists. A baby feels hunger: well, there is such a thing as food. A duckling wants to swim: well, there is such a thing as water. . . . If I find in myself a desire which no experience in this world can satisfy, the most probable explanation is that I was made for another world. If none of my earthly pleasures satisfy it, that does not prove that the universe is a fraud. Probably earthly pleasures were never meant to satisfy it, but only to arouse it, to suggest the real thing.

—C. S. LEWIS, *Mere Christianity,* p. 120, MacMillan, NY, 1979

Here are some other desires and their means of fulfillment:

DESIRE	FULFILLMENT
thirst	water
knowledge	information
companionship	people
children	procreation
accomplishment	success
recognition	awards

§ Can you think of others to add to the list?

DESIRE	FULFILLMENT

§ Besides the deep-down thirst Kyle was talking about, can you think of a desire for which there is no fulfillment on earth?

3. Kyle suggested five ways we could view the possible fulfillment of our deepest thirst. As you approach this study, how would you describe your attitude? Would you say you are more cynical, skeptical, curious, settled, or satisfied?

☐ Cynical—certain that pretty much everything is a scam

☐ Skeptical—suspicious of everything (politicians, preachers, even your own brother!) and need clear proof before trusting anything

☐ Curious—interested in finding truth and open to whatever it may be

☐ Settled—fairly content but knowing that your deepest longings are not being met

☐ Satisfied—certain you have found what you are looking for and, as a result, thoroughly fulfilled

§ Why do you say so?

4. Do you really believe Mandi lost her wedding ring in the ocean and then Vince and Kyle found it later with an underwater metal detector in near total darkness?

☐ "No way! That has to be bogus."

☐ "It's doubtful. I'd have to see some convincing proof."

☐ "It's possible. I'd be interested in hearing more about it."

☐ "Who cares? What does it matter?"

☐ "I'm not sure, but I do know I've had equally thrilling experiences in my life."

If you said . . .

☐ "No way! What a fake," then you are probably a cynic.

☐ "It's doubtful. I'd have to see more proof," then you are probably a skeptic.

☐ "That's interesting. I'd like to hear more about it," then you are probably curious.

☐ "Who cares? What does it matter?" then you are probably someone who settles for what you have and doesn't look for more.

☐ "I'm not sure it's true, but I've had thrilling things happen in my life," then you are most likely learning to be satisfied.

§ Do you find this assessment to be an accurate gauge of your attitude toward new information in life?

5. What do you think is the likelihood that Jesus can fill a person's deepest thirst? What makes you think so?

REFLECTION

These are optional thought questions to ponder or respond to in writing between sessions. You will *not* be asked to share your answers in the next session, but you may find it helpful to talk them over with a friend.

1. Is there anything you picked up from the DVD or group time that you would like to think more about or be sure to remember?

2. Try to describe your own deep thirst, if you feel you have one.

3. Do you experience this thirst at certain times more than others? If so, when are those times of intensified thirst?

4. Why might you feel this thirst more at these times?

5. What have you found to be the thirst-quenching ability of the items listed below? Circle your answers.

Money	Zero	Low	Medium	High	Complete
Possessions	Zero	Low	Medium	High	Complete
Success	Zero	Low	Medium	High	Complete
Relationships	Zero	Low	Medium	High	Complete

6. When you do get thirsty in the deeper sense, what do you generally turn to in order to quench your thirst? Describe how well it works.

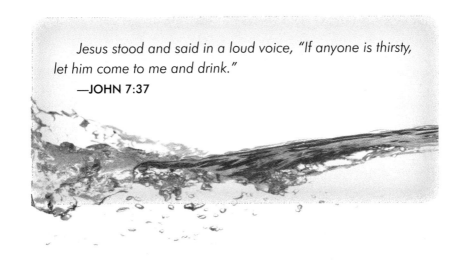

Jesus stood and said in a loud voice, "If anyone is thirsty, let him come to me and drink."
—JOHN 7:37

LESSON

2

Polluted

THE POISON OF RELIGION

≈ DISCUSSION ≈

1. Kyle used words like *boring, outdated,* and *hypocritical* to describe a lot of people's experience of church. What words would you use to describe your experience of church?

2. If you had to describe Jesus from your church experience alone, what would you say He is like? How close do you think this church view of Jesus is to the real Jesus?

3. When Kyle went door to door asking people why they didn't attend church, he found that most people didn't say things like, "I don't believe in God" or "I think the Bible is a bunch of fairy tales." Instead, he heard things like, "Church is boring" or "I don't understand what the preacher is talking about" or "I'm busy."

§ When it comes to faith, would you say your primary problem is with Jesus and what He is like or with the church and what it is like? It could be with both, but if it is both, with which do you have a bigger struggle—Jesus or the church?

4. One of the perversions of Christianity is turning it into a bunch of rules. When Kyle was talking about this, he listed some old laws that were pretty funny.

   § Which of these laws do you think should still be on the books?

FOR	AGAINST	
	✓	A person may not wear cowboy boots unless he owns at least three cows.
	✓	Owners of homes with Christmas lights up past February 2 will be fined $250.
✓		Gathering and consuming roadkill shall be illegal.
	✓	No more than five inoperable vehicles may occupy one piece of property at one time.
	✓	A woman may not buy a hat without her husband's permission.
	✓	Women should not be allowed to drive motorized vehicles unless a man precedes them waving a red flag to warn oncoming pedestrians or motorists.

5. There are a lot of dos and do nots in the Bible, and that is why a lot of people think being a Christian is all about following rules. But the Bible says that one reason God gave all these rules was to make it clear that people cannot follow all the rules—that perfect rule-based living is impossible.

> *Now do you see it? No one can ever be made right in God's sight by doing what the law commands. For the more we know of God's laws, the clearer it becomes that we aren't obeying them.*
> **—ROMANS 3:20 TLB**
>
> *So what was the law for? It was given to show that the wrong things people do are against God's will. . . . In other words, the law was our guardian leading us to Christ.*
> **—GALATIANS 3:19, 24 NCV**

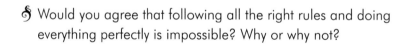

§ Would you agree that following all the right rules and doing everything perfectly is impossible? Why or why not?

Reba

6. Besides rule-based living, Kyle mentioned other distortions of Jesus' message. He talked about what one writer termed "Christianity and _____"; that is, stuff added to Jesus like political and social agendas, or even personal opinions. He said such additions are like nasty ranchero sauce added to a good burrito.

§ What have you seen added to the basic message of Jesus?

7. In the DVD, the minister reads Luke 15:1–2 from the Bible:

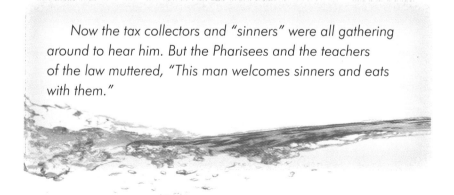

Now the tax collectors and "sinners" were all gathering around to hear him. But the Pharisees and the teachers of the law muttered, "This man welcomes sinners and eats with them."

H2O A JOURNEY OF FAITH   *Luke 19-10*

§ The religious leaders of His day saw Jesus as a person who readily connected with those whom others viewed as immoral. How close is this description to your view of Jesus? Would you say pretty close? Or quite distant? Why?

8. Are you willing to consider Jesus on His own terms, apart from how today's church might represent Him?

~ REFLECTION ~

1. Of the pollutants Kyle mentioned, which has particularly bothered you?

   _____ the boring, monotonous nature of so many churches

   _____ making following Jesus all about keeping certain rules

   _____ political or social agendas, and personal opinions added onto Jesus' message

   _____ the hypocrisy of those who claim to be following Him

   _____ the general weirdness of Christians

   _____ something else: _____

2. If you had an important message to tell the world, but other people came along and twisted, polluted, and added to it, how would you feel?

3. What would you imagine to be Jesus' reaction to the abuses and misuses of His message?

4. The Bible actually tells us to not blindly trust people, *especially* those who claim to be communicating messages from God. That's because people will let us down. People will intentionally mislead. People are polluted. John, one of Jesus' closest followers, wrote:

> *My dear friends, don't believe everything you hear. Carefully weigh and examine what people tell you. Not everyone who talks about God comes from God. There are a lot of lying preachers loose in the world.*
> **—1 JOHN 4:1 MSG**

 Try writing out your view of Jesus; that is, try to describe Him as you see Him.

5. Where did you get your information for what you just wrote? Check all that apply.

_____ from accounts of Him recorded in the Bible

_____ from what I've read in books or magazines

_____ from how the church represents Him

_____ from the way Christians act

_____ from the attitudes of my parents, professors, friends, etc.

 Which aspects of your view came from eyewitness descriptions of Him like those found in the Bible? Circle them.

 Which came from less-than-reliable sources? Cross them out.

 Which came from . . . well, you don't know where? Put a question mark beside those.

6. The preacher in the DVD described Jesus this way.

- The love of Jesus is not conditional.

- It isn't based on ulterior motives.

- It has no hidden agendas.

- There's nothing you can do to deserve it.

- And there's nothing you can do to lose it.

- It's free. It's powerful. It's pure.

§ Are you willing to consider Jesus on His own terms, to see if He is like what this preacher described?

Never will I leave you; never will I forsake you.
—**HEBREWS 13:5**

NOTES

3

Source

THE GOD WHO LOVES

~~ DISCUSSION ~~

1. Who did you find yourself identifying with, or resonating with, most: the Korean American girl, her mother, Kyle's daughter, or Kyle as the good dad?

2. What is your reaction to the fact that the most common descriptive name for God in the New Testament is "Father"?

3. Here are some descriptive words for God based on the Bible.

✓ Check those you believe are absolutely true of God.

X Mark an X beside those you believe are NOT true of God.

? Place a question mark beside those about which you just aren't sure.

___ living (alive)	___ infinite (no beginning or end)	___ eternal
___ omnipotent (all-powerful)	___ omniscient (all-knowing)	___ omnipresent (present everywhere)
___ holy (perfect)	___ wise	___ impartial
___ loving	___ patient	___ compassionate
___ forgiving	___ faithful	___ generous
___ kind	___ responsive	___ personal

Total checkmarks in shaded area: _____

Total in unshaded area: _____

4. One inaccurate view of God is that of an angry father. You may wonder why negative words such as *angry* are not on this list describing God. While anger may be a temporary reaction to evil, a reaction that flows out of God's holiness, anger is not an ongoing characteristic of God as He is in and of Himself. Look at the Scripture below:

> *His anger lasts only a moment, but his favor lasts a lifetime.*
> **—PSALM 30:5**

A good parent might sometimes get angry, but anger is not who he or she is. That's how the Bible describes God: He may get angry, but He is not angry in the same way He is loving or kind.

🎵 Do you think this distinction between what God sometimes does and what He is in and of Himself is valid? Why or why not?

5. Mark a D at the place on each line that depicts how you experienced your dad when you were little, say, in elementary school. If you didn't have a dad, choose the closest person you had to a father figure.

⑤ Next put a G on each line at the place that represents how you see God these days.

Gentle	___	___	___	G	___	D	___	___	Stern
Close	___	___	___	___	___	___	___	___	Distant
Talkative	___	___	___	___	___	___	___	___	Silent
Patient	___	___	___	___	___	___	___	___	Explosive
Joyful	___	___	___	___	___	___	___	___	Somber
Encouraging	___	___	___	___	___	___	___	___	Critical
Interested	___	___	___	___	___	___	___	___	Apathetic
Kind	___	___	___	___	___	___	___	___	Harsh
Honest	___	___	___	___	___	___	___	___	Deceitful
Consistent	___	___	___	___	___	___	___	___	Erratic

⑤ How is your experience of your dad when you were a kid similar to how you see God now? What does this exercise show you, if anything?

6. Would you welcome or resist the concept of a loving heavenly Father? Why?

7. What impact would it make on your life if you did see God as a patient, loving, forgiving Father?

~ REFLECTION ~

1. During the group discussion, you were asked to mark which of the characteristics of God seem true to you, which seem false, and which you were unsure of. Look at them again, but this time think of them in terms of which ones you *experience* as you relate to God. For instance, you may think that God is kind, but you may not experience this kindness when you try to relate to Him.

E Place an *E* beside those you experience personally

B Place a *B* beside those you believe but do *not* experience

___ living (alive)	___ infinite (no beginning or end)	___ eternal
___ omnipotent (all-powerful)	___ omniscient (all-knowing)	___ omnipresent (present everywhere)
___ holy (perfect)	___ wise	___ impartial
___ loving	___ patient	___ compassionate
___ forgiving	___ faithful	___ generous
___ kind	___ responsive	___ personal

§ What did this exercise reveal to you, if anything?

2. Here are some reasons a person may resist the idea of God being a loving Father. If you find yourself pushing away any thought of a loving heavenly Father, do any of these lie beneath that resistance?

____ I just don't believe it's possible that God is like that.

____ I feel so unworthy of that kind of love.

____ I used to believe it, but too many bad things have happened to me.

____ I've been burned too many times when I've trusted someone to be loving.

____ I don't want to believe in a God of any kind, because that would mean I have to do things His way.

____ I am uncomfortable with the experience or feeling of love. It's just too . . . squishy!

____ Other: _____

3. You might want to slowly make your way through these Scriptures that highlight God as Father. Underline anything that stands out to you.

A father to the fatherless, a defender of widows, is God in his holy dwelling.
—PSALM 68:5

Which of you, if his son asks for bread, will give him a stone? Or if he asks for a fish, will give him a snake? If you, then, though you are evil, know how to give good gifts to your children, how much more will your Father in heaven give good gifts to those who ask him!
—**MATTHEW 7:9–11**

One day Jesus was praying in a certain place. When he finished, one of his disciples said to him, "Lord, teach us to pray, just as John taught his disciples." He said to them, "When you pray, say: "'Father, . . .'"
—**LUKE 11:1–2**

For you did not receive a spirit that makes you a slave again to fear, but you received the Spirit of sonship. And by him we cry, "Abba, Father." The Spirit himself testifies with our spirit that we are God's children.
—**ROMANS 8:15–16 (Abba is Aramaic for "Daddy")**

Give praise to the God and Father of our Lord Jesus Christ! He is the Father who gives tender love. All comfort comes from him.
—**2 CORINTHIANS 1:3–4 NIRV**

I will be a Father to you, and you will be my sons and daughters, says the Lord Almighty.
—**2 CORINTHIANS 6:18**

You have forgotten that word of hope. It speaks to you as children. It says, "My son, think of the Lord's training as important. Do not lose hope when he corrects you. The Lord trains those he loves. He punishes everyone he accepts as a son."

—HEBREWS 12:5–6 NIRV

How great is the love the Father has lavished on us, that we should be called children of God! And that is what we are!

—1 JOHN 3:1

4. Could you talk to a fatherly God like these passages describe? If you are willing, try it.

LESSON

4

Pure

THE ULTIMATE SATISFACTION

∼DISCUSSION∼

1. How did you find yourself relating to the woman in the story?
   Did you find yourself liking her, disliking her, connecting with her,
   criticizing her?

§ What do you think she was thirsting for in her life?

2. This may be a dangerous question, but in your experience can relationships with other people fulfill the deepest thirsts in our lives?

3. Jesus said He came to:

- proclaim good news to the poor

- announce freedom for prisoners

- bring recovery of sight to the blind

- release the oppressed

Luke 19-4

§ This claim is recorded in Luke 4. Which needs can you relate to personally?

- Poor: feeling destitute materially, emotionally, relationally, or spiritually

- Captive: boxed in or controlled by others such as your parents, your past, your work situation, or just society in general

- Blind: unable to see clearly, make sense of it all, or figure out how to make life work

- Oppressed: dominated or tormented by inner demons, addictions, anger, or forces that seem to be more powerful than you

4. Which do you sense is most likely to provide you the freedom or power you are looking for to satisfy your deepest needs?

_____ Rules: a solid system of dos and do nots

_____ Stuff: a lot of inanimate material possessions

__2__ People: relationships with other human beings

__1__ God: a relationship with a divine being

_____ Self: something within, yet untapped

_____ Combination: a mixture of some or all of the above

§ Why do you think so?

5. Kyle claimed that Jesus knows everything about you, yet still loves you. "The one who knows you the best loves you the most."

§ Do you think this is possible? If not, what makes it hard to believe?

6. Kyle tells his story of guacamole. Some of us told our own stories of foods we used to despise but now enjoy.

   § What's the possibility that you have been disliking Jesus, when in reality, if you really knew Him, you would enjoy what He offers?

7. Some religious leaders say, "I will show you the way to truth so you can have real life." Jesus says, "I am the way and the truth and the life" (John 14:6). In another place, He said, "I am the bread of life. He who comes to me will never go hungry, and he who believes in me will never be thirsty" (John 6:35).

   § What do you think of this claim?

8. Complete this sentence: "I believe Jesus (can/cannot/might be able to) quench my thirst because . . ."

~ REFLECTION ~

1. Which of these statements rings true to you?

_____ Jesus can't help me.

_____ Jesus wants nothing to do with me.

_____ Jesus is making an offer too good to be true.

_____ Jesus is more interested in me being good than in me myself.

_____ Jesus is interested in me even though He knows all about me.

2. Try reading the whole story of Jesus and the woman of Samaria as told in John 4. As you do, underline anything that stands out or that you have questions about.

> Now he had to go through Samaria. So he came to a town in Samaria called Sychar, near the plot of ground Jacob had given to his son Joseph. Jacob's well was there, and Jesus, tired as he was from the journey, sat down by the well. It was about the sixth hour.
>
> When a Samaritan woman came to draw water, Jesus said to her, "Will you give me a drink?" (His disciples had gone into the town to buy food.) The Samaritan woman said to him, "You are a Jew and I am a Samaritan woman. How can you ask me for a drink?" (For Jews do not associate with Samaritans.)
>
> Jesus answered her, "If you knew the gift of God and who it is that asks you for a drink, you would have asked him and he would have given you living water."
>
> "Sir," the woman said, "you have nothing to draw with and the well is deep. Where can you get this living water? Are you greater than our father Jacob, who gave us the well and drank from it himself, as did also his sons and his flocks and herds?"
>
> Jesus answered, "Everyone who drinks this water will be thirsty again, but whoever drinks the water I give him will never thirst. Indeed, the water I give him will become in him a spring of water welling up to eternal life."
>
> The woman said to him, "Sir, give me this water so that I won't get thirsty and have to keep coming here to draw water."
>
> He told her, "Go, call your husband and come back."
>
> "I have no husband," she replied.

Jesus said to her, "You are right when you say you have no husband. The fact is, you have had five husbands, and the man you now have is not your husband. What you have just said is quite true."

"Sir," the woman said, "I can see that you are a prophet. Our fathers worshiped on this mountain, but you Jews claim that the place where we must worship is in Jerusalem."

Jesus declared, "Believe me, woman, a time is coming when you will worship the Father neither on this mountain nor in Jerusalem. You Samaritans worship what you do not know; we worship what we do know, for salvation is from the Jews. Yet a time is coming and has now come when the true worshipers will worship the Father in spirit and truth, for they are the kind of worshipers the Father seeks. God is spirit, and his worshipers must worship in spirit and in truth."

The woman said, "I know that Messiah (called Christ) is coming." "When he comes, he will explain everything to us."

Then Jesus declared, "I who speak to you am he."

Just then his disciples returned and were surprised to find him talking with a woman. But no one asked, "What do you want?" or "Why are you talking with her?"

Then, leaving her water jar, the woman went back to the town and said to the people, "Come, see a man who told me everything I ever did. Could this be the Christ?" They came out of the town and made their way toward him. . . .

Many of the Samaritans from that town believed in him because of the woman's testimony, "He told me everything I ever did." So when the Samaritans came to him, they urged him to stay with them, and he stayed two days. And because of his words many more became believers.

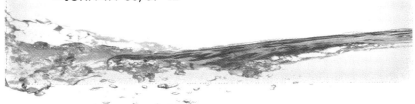

*They said to the woman, "We no longer believe just
because of what you said; now we have heard for ourselves,
and we know that this man really is the Savior of the world."*
—JOHN 4:4–30, 39–42

3. Based on what you just read, would Jesus be the kind of person
you would like to know?

____ Yes!   ____ No!   ____ Maybe

✑ Why or why not?

If you would like to know more about Jesus, try reading one
of the accounts of His life found in the Bible books of Matthew,
Mark, Luke, or John. Start with any of them; they are all good! Use
a modern translation that's understandable. If you have a Bible
that is difficult to understand, buy a more up-to-date version. Your
H2O leader can probably help you choose a good translation.
Oftentimes, writing out our thoughts helps us clarify our thinking.

4. Now that you have had four weeks of study, what thoughts or questions do you have about Jesus?

I am the way and the truth and the life.
—JESUS, JOHN 14:6

NOTES

LESSON 5

Mirage

THE SEARCH FOR MORE

DISCUSSION

1. Have you ever believed that a certain thing—a car, job, or person—would fulfill you if only you could get it? If you did get it, what was it like? Was it everything you imagined it would be?

2. Do you believe that if, like Solomon, you had just about everything you wanted that you, too, would end up saying, "Meaningless! Meaningless!" (Ecclesiastes 1:2)? Why or why not?

3. In your experience, what can possessions do for you, and what can't they do for you?

4. In your experience, what can achievement give you and what can't it give you?

5. How about relationships? What have you found that they can do for you and what can't they do for you?

6. The purposes Jesus offers us are to know God and live with Him forever as well as to participate in the mission of helping others know God and live with Him forever. How would you compare those purposes with the usual purposes people pursue in life, such as getting rich, raising happy kids, building a big company, or even finding a cure for cancer?

7. How about the security Jesus offers? He says He can guarantee that those who come to Him will never perish, that He can grant them eternal life. Do you think there is life after death, and if so, what do you think it is like? What do you think of Jesus' offer to give ongoing life?

8. It was also claimed that Jesus offers unconditional love, that is, He loves everyone regardless of what they are like. How does this compare to the kind of love you have experienced in the world?

Romans 5-8

1 John 4:8   Page 1364

acts 17:11

John 8:31-32   Page 1177

conclusion

NOT even close

~~REFLECTION~~

1. "If I only had . . . , then I'd be happy!" How would you complete that sentence? If you only had a mate? If you only had a boatload of money? If you could only find the right career? Or maybe it's something as simple as "If I could only get the house cleaned up, the checkbook straightened out, and the kids to school on time!" How would you finish the sentence?

"If I only had _____ , then I'd be happy!"

"If I only had _____ , then I'd be happy!"

"If I only had _____ , then I'd be happy!"

"If I only had _____ , then I'd be happy!"

"If I only had _____ , then I'd be happy!"

2. Is what you are pursuing in an effort to make yourself happy poisoning your life in some way? For example, you might be pursuing corporate success, but it is leading to ulcers and a shaky marriage. Or you might be going from one sexual relationship to another, but this is causing emptiness and regret. Identify any damaging effects to which your efforts to quench your thirst are leading.

3. Consider the following Scripture.

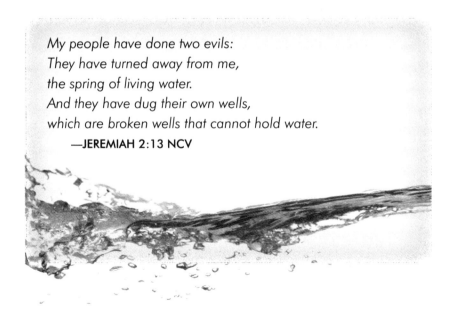

My people have done two evils:
They have turned away from me,
the spring of living water.
And they have dug their own wells,
which are broken wells that cannot hold water.
    —JEREMIAH 2:13 NCV

§ Are our wells really broken?

§ Alfred Adler (psychologist and author) said that everyone needs purpose. What if a person had it all—lots of possessions, great achievements, good looks, and meaningful relationships? Is that enough to provide all the purpose someone would need in life?

§ What about the security Carl Jung (psychologist and anthropologist) said we all need? If we had it all, would that supply all the security we would want?

§ Sigmund Freud (originator of psychoanalysis) said we need love. Would having it all deliver all the love that a human being could ever need?

4. Jesus claims to offer living water, pure water. Based on what you know at this point, how would you describe what He is offering?

_____ radiator fluid: it's actually poison, the opiate of the people

_____ placebo water: it makes people think they are getting better but it's just a mirage

_____ tonic water: it helps; it is good but not necessarily better than other drinks

_____ living water: it's the only "good stuff" that can satisfy the deepest thirst

5. Here are some Scriptures that are referred to in the DVD presentation. Circle anything that stands out to you.

The words of the Teacher, son of David, king in Jerusalem:

> *"Meaningless! Meaningless!"*
>   *says the Teacher.*
> *"Utterly meaningless!*
>   *Everything is meaningless."*
> *What does man gain from all his labor*
>   *at which he toils under the sun? . . .*
> *All things are wearisome,*
>   *more than one can say.*
> *The eye never has enough of seeing,*
>   *nor the ear its fill of hearing.*
> **—ECCLESIASTES 1:1–3, 8**

I thought in my heart, "Come now, I will test you with pleasure to find out what is good." But that also proved to be meaningless. "Laughter," I said, "is foolish. And what does pleasure accomplish?" I tried cheering myself with wine, and embracing folly—my mind still guiding me with wisdom. I wanted to see what was worthwhile for men to do under heaven during the few days of their lives.

I undertook great projects: I built houses for myself and planted vineyards. I made gardens and parks and planted all kinds of fruit trees in them. I made reservoirs to water groves of flourishing trees. I bought male and female slaves and had other slaves who were born in my house. I also owned more herds and flocks than anyone in Jerusalem before me. I amassed silver and gold for myself, and the treasure of kings and provinces. I acquired men and women singers, and a harem as well—the delights of the heart of man. I became greater by far than anyone in Jerusalem before me. In all this my wisdom stayed with me.

I denied myself nothing my eyes desired; I refused my heart no pleasure.

My heart took delight in all my work, and this was the reward for all my labor.

Yet when I surveyed all that my hands had done and what I had toiled to achieve, everything was meaningless, a chasing after the wind; nothing was gained under the sun.

—ECCLESIASTES 2:1–11

Can anything ever separate us from Christ's love? Does it mean he no longer loves us if we have trouble or calamity, or are persecuted, or are hungry or cold or in danger or threatened with death? (Even the Scriptures say, "For your sake we are killed every day; we are being slaughtered like sheep.") No, despite all these things, overwhelming victory is ours through Christ, who loved us. And I am convinced that nothing can ever separate us from his love.

Death can't, and life can't. The angels can't, and the demons can't. Our fears for today, our worries about tomorrow, and even the powers of hell can't keep God's love away. Whether we are high above the sky or in the deepest ocean, nothing in all creation will ever be able to separate us from the love of God that is revealed in Christ Jesus our Lord.

—ROMANS 8:35–39 NLT

The Spirit and the bride say, "Come!" And let him who hears say, "Come!" Whoever is thirsty, let him come; and whoever wishes, let him take the free gift of the water of life.

—REVELATION 22:17

6. You may have tried talking to God before. Would you be willing to try writing your thoughts to Him? In a sense, it's just like writing a letter. Write what comes to mind. You may find it therapeutic.

Ò God,
Here are some of my thoughts . . .

NOTES

LESSON 6

Drowning

THE PLAN OF SALVATION

DISCUSSION

_ml_

1. What are your feelings after watching this segment?

Regardless of what we do, No matter what sin, what vices we have, No matter _How_ Far we walk away from Jesus He makes away for us to come back to him _IF_ we Except & Believe ~~But + Hard~~ ~~And~~ We have Become so dry we don't Even see what He provides For us We Just Stumble Throug what He gives to save us!

2. Has anyone ever paid your tab or saved you from a mess you couldn't get yourself out of? If so, what was that like for you? How did you find yourself responding to their efforts?

3. What do you think the chances are that God would do something like that for people on earth?

4. Kyle brought up the dreadful Bible word: sin. Do you believe there is such a thing as sin, that is, real wrongdoing?

5. Kyle mentioned four ways people deal with their ugly stuff, their sin.

   • One is to deny it, to just not face it.

   • Another is to rationalize it away. They say things like, "I have a right to be happy; I'm not hurting anybody; I couldn't help it." Someone said that when we rationalize, we are actually telling ourselves "rational lies."

   • Another is to compare themselves with those who are worse— "At least I'm not as bad as so-and-so!"

   • The last is that people try to hide their bad habits—they stash their drug paraphernalia or never tell anyone the hateful thoughts in their heads.

§ Do you think Kyle is right? If so, why do people do these things?

6. One of the big questions about Christianity is, Why does God allow a hell? If a person rebelled against God, wouldn't submit to God, what do you think God should do with such a person?

_____ Let him into heaven anyway (but then God would be letting sin into His perfection and immediately polluting it).

_____ Force this person to surrender (but this would violate his free will, robbing him of his right to choose).

_____ Give the person his wish (but this would mean separation from God and all that is good, that is, existence in outer darkness, or hell).

_____ Create a nice place where sinful, unsubmissive people could go and continue to be sinful and unsubmissive but be as happy as they can be in this state (but this would violate God's justice and be unfair to those who had gone all out to do what was right).

_____ Just annihilate him (but then he wouldn't pay for the wrongs he did commit; people could literally "get away with murder").

7. What did you think of the illustration of the two glasses of water? What do you think God should do with the dark stuff in people's cups?

8. Read Luke 23:33.

> *When they came to the place called the Skull, there they crucified him, along with the criminals—one on his right, the other on his left.*

§ What stands out to you from this reading?

9. This verse tells what happened to Jesus. But why did it happen? Look at Mark 10:45 (NIRV):

Even the Son of Man did not come to be served. Instead, he came to serve others. He came to give his life as the price for setting many people free.

ᛠ Jesus is speaking in this verse. When He uses the title "Son of Man," He is referring to Himself. So what stands out to you from this verse?

10. In the book of Isaiah, we find a prophecy, a sort of advance notification from God about what He was going to do in the future. This was written about seven hundred years before Jesus' time. But it describes what Jesus would do.

> He suffered the things we should have suffered.
> He took on himself the pain that should have been ours.
> But we thought God was punishing him.
> We thought God was wounding him and making him suffer.
> But the servant was pierced because we had sinned.
> He was crushed because we had done what was evil.
> He was punished to make us whole again.
> His wounds have healed us.
> All of us are like sheep.
> We have wandered away from God.
> All of us have turned to our own way.
> And the Lord has placed on his servant the sins of all of us.
> **—ISAIAH 53:4–6 NIRV**

§ What do you think of this idea of Jesus giving His life to pay the tab for our messing up?

REFLECTION

1. What we suggest here may be difficult. But to get an honest assessment of your situation, you might decide to try it despite the difficulty.

   To make the most of this time, have a glass half filled with clean water, and a cup of black coffee, cola, or some other dark drink.

   Make a list of the bad stuff you've done. Think about different stages of your life—childhood, high school, college, your young adult years, and so on. Write down whatever unkind, selfish, or harmful things that strike you. It may be as "small" as teasing the neighborhood nerd or stealing pocket change from your mom's purse. It may be as "big" as getting your girlfriend pregnant or screaming profanities at your kids. Take your time. Don't rush. You won't have to show this page to anyone. So whatever comes to mind, write it down.

2. James 4:17 says, "Well, remember that if a man knows what is right and fails to do it, his failure is a real sin" (PHILLIPS).

   If this is true, then what "failure-sins" would you have to add to your list? What should you have done in each stage of life, but didn't? Helped your mom more? Been nice to the neighborhood nerd? Volunteered your time for some worthy cause? Spent time building up your kids? Again, take your time. Mull over things you knew you should have done but neglected.

♪ How do you feel about your list? What is your reaction?

3. If a person did something wrong just five times a day—tell a white lie, gossip about a coworker, blow up at the kids, ignore the nudge to do something good, like call Mom or encourage a friend—in fifty years this person would have accumulated more than ninety thousand offenses!

   ◌ Would you guess your average number of shortcomings per day to be less than or more than five?

   ____ less than five ____ more than five ____ way more than five!

4. Take your glass of clean water. Add to it the amount of coffee or cola that you think represents how much bad stuff you have done in your life. Try to be honest. (If you're not honest then you have to add "dishonesty" to your list too!)

   ◌ So, how dark is your cup?

   ◌ What will you do with the dark stuff inside?

5. Look back over the Scriptures that were read during the discussion (Luke 23:33; Mark 10:45; Isaiah 53:4–6). What are these passages saying to you now?

Keep your glass and its contents as a visual reminder until our next session. If you are willing, bring it with you to the next gathering.

LESSON

7

Drink

THE NEW BEGINNING

∼DISCUSSION∼

1. What are your thoughts and feelings after watching this episode? What questions do you have?

2. Which is closest to how you have responded to God's free offer of a pardon and new life?

- I don't believe it.

- I don't need it.

- I'll try to earn it.

- I don't understand it.

- I don't want it.

- I'll simply accept it.

♪ Put your response to what Jesus is offering in your own words.

3. How are you responding to this offer of a new life?

4. In Kyle's prayer, he mentioned several ways to express new faith in Jesus.

   a. Reject your old way of thinking and acting that was outside God's will. You see your old ways as wrong and decide to do things God's way as best you can. Nobody can do this perfectly, but you decide to try. The Bible calls this *repentance* (Acts 3:19; 17:30; 26:20).

   b. *Confession* is simply saying aloud that you believe Jesus is Lord (Matthew 10:32; Romans 10:9–10; 1 Timothy 6:12–14). In a sense, confession is what you just did when you told this group that you decided to trust Jesus.

   c. *Baptism* is when a person is dipped under water. It is a picture of dying to your old self, of burying your past, being totally cleansed of all your guilt, and being raised up to a new kind of life (Romans 6:3–4; Galatians 3:26–27; 1 Peter 3:20–22). Back when Jesus' first followers were around and the New Testament was being written, a person was always baptized soon after he or she decided to trust Jesus (Acts 2:40–41; 8:26–40; 16:16–30).

   ⸮ Does it make sense how these steps can help a person latch on to, or unwrap, God's free gift of salvation?

5. Look at the words to the song "Amazing Grace" printed below. As you listen to and read the lyrics, if you feel moved to do so, please feel free to exchange your dirty glass of water for a fresh one under the cross.

Amazing grace! How sweet the sound
That saved a wretch like me!
I once was lost, but now I'm found;
Was blind, but now I see.

'Twas grace that taught my heart to fear,
And grace my fear relieved;
How precious did that grace appear
The hour I first believed!

Through many dangers, toils and snares,
I have already come;
'Tis grace hath brought me safe thus far,
And grace will lead me home.

When we've been there ten thousand years,
Bright shining as the sun,
We've no less days to sing God's praise
Than when we'd first begun.
   —JOHN NEWTON, 1779

6. For those of you who exchanged your glasses at the cross, how did that feel? What was your reaction?

~ REFLECTION ~

1. Do you have a sense that you have met God or interacted with Him in some way during your H2O experience? If so, what was that like? What did you make of it?

2. Where do you see yourself going next in your spiritual journey?

3. If you are not ready to accept Jesus' free offer of forgiveness of sins and escape from the death penalty, what's the reason?

_____ I don't think the offer is real.

_____ I don't need the help; I'm not that bad.

_____ I refuse to accept anyone's charity; I should pay for my own mistakes.

_____ I just feel too guilty to believe that I can ever be released from my guilt.

_____ I know I can't live up to it; I'll end up going back to my old ways.

_____ Other: _____

4. The following passages of Scripture have been paraphrased for this exercise. They describe what Jesus has done for us and what it means for us. Personalize them by writing your name in each of the blanks.

When they came to the place called the Skull, there they crucified him, along with the criminals—one on his right, the other on his left.
Jesus said, "Father, forgive _____ , for _____ does not know what he or she is doing."
—LUKE 23:33–34

For God so loved _____ that he gave his one and only Son, that if _____ believes in him _____ shall not perish but have eternal life.
—JOHN 3:16

God saved _____ by his special favor when _____ believed.
And _____ can't take credit for this; it is a gift from God.
Salvation is not a reward for the good things _____ has done, so none of us including _____ can boast about it.
For _____ is God's masterpiece.
He has created _____ anew in Christ Jesus, so that _____ can do the good things he planned for _____ long ago.
—EPHESIANS 2:8–10 NLT

Christ never sinned but God put _____'s *sin on Him.*

Then _____ *is made right with God because of what Christ has done for* _____ .

—2 CORINTHIANS 5:21 NLV

5. Try reading these passages aloud with your name in them. What is that like?

If you would like to find out what happened after Jesus' death, read Luke 24.

~NOTES~

The Easter Experience

H20:
A Journey of Faith

FOLLOWER'S OUTREACH KIT

A Journey of Faith

FOLLOWER'S
OUTREACH KIT

Not A Fan
A Follower's Story

not a fan.

not a fan.

kyle idleman

becoming a completely.
committed. follower.
kyle idleman